Early praise for *The Dance of the Possible*:

"You'll find a lot to steal from this short, inspiring guide to being creative. Made me want to get up and make stuff!" - **Austin Kleon, author of** *How To Steal Like An Artist*

"A fun, funny, no-BS guide to finding new ideas and finishing them. Instantly useful." - **Ramez Naam, author of the** *Nexus* **trilogy**

"Concisely debunks all kinds of misconceptions about the creative process in a book that's no-nonsense, fun, and inspiring." - **Mason Currey, author of** *Daily Rituals: How Artists Work*

"If I were alive I'd consider endorsing this book, but would likely just tear it apart with my chisel and get back to work." - **Michelangelo, creator of** *David,* **the Sistine Chapel ceiling (including** *The Creation of Adam* **fresco) and other works**

"This book will undoubtedly increase your abilities to invent, innovate, inspire, and make things that matter. It's fun, it's funny, and it's phenomenally effective." - **Jane McGonigal, author of** *The New York Times* ... ıd *SuperBetter*

"...makes the font of creativity something that is right at your door, offering you a cup and inviting you to drink every day."
- **Andrew McMasters, Founder and Artistic Director, Jet City Improv**

"The best short book on creativity yet! Playful, irreverent, insightful, exciting! Full of good advice delivered by example rather than description. Get on with it, Berkun advises, and expeditiously gets you on your way!" - **Bob Root-Bernstein, co-author of *Sparks of Genius*, Professor of Physiology, Michigan State University**

"...demystifies the creative process and makes it easily accessible to anyone. If you're looking for the quickest route from stuck to creative spark, this is the book for you."
– **Dave Gray, author of *Liminal Thinking* and *The Connected Company***

"A spirited and tangibly useful guide to actually getting art done — memorably clear, mercifully artspeak-free, and filled with pithy nuggets of real-world wisdom." - **Ted Orland, co-author of *Art & Fear*.**

""I've been inspired by Scott Berkun's creativity for over a decade. In *Dance of the Possible*, I finally got to see how he does it." – **Jake Knapp, author of *The Wall Street Journal bestseller Sprint* and Design Partner at Google Ventures**

THE DANCE
OF THE
POSSIBLE

....

THE MOSTLY HONEST AND COMPLETELY IRREVERENT GUIDE TO CREATIVITY

BY SCOTT BERKUN

COVER AND ILLUSTRATIONS
BY TIM KORDIK

Dance of The Possible/ Scott Berkun -- 1st ed.
ISBN 978-0-9838731-4-3
March 2017, RC8

Table of Contents

A truly brief introduction

Part One

Part Two

A TRULY BRIEF INTRODUCTION

(THE PAGE BEFORE THE OTHER PAGES)

....

For years I've taught people about ideas and how they work. In lectures and at whiteboards around the world I've experimented with different ways to teach lessons on creative thinking, trying to be more concise and useful each time. I've discovered there isn't that much to know: perhaps a few well-explained insights, just enough to fill a short and worthy book, which is what I hope you find in the pages that follow.

PART
ONE

1. THE SOURCE

Where does creativity come from? This sounds like an important question, but the first surprise of this book is that it's not. To prove this, I've listed some possible answers based on the latest neuroscience research on creative thinking. If you guess the right answer to my question, which I doubt you will, I will give you a special and wonderful prize. Choose wisely.

Creativity comes from:

A) Friendly aliens living underground in the planet Saturn
B) The tasty filling found inside blueberry doughnuts
C) An invisible gas that is released only when you finish a nice bottle of wine
D) All of the above
E) Some of the above (there are no aliens on Saturn)

Of course these answers are both made up and wrong. I admit that I hoped C was true, but even after many experiments I was never able to stay awake long enough to see the gas, if it exists. I promise I will keep trying, as with the pursuit of all interesting ideas, persistence is required.

Meanwhile, the only possibly correct answer is F) Your mind. This seems obvious, yet when people decide they want to be more creative, they are willing to look just about anywhere except inside themselves. I know from years of study that most of what you need you already have, despite the books, seminars and coaches that claim otherwise. I admit this is a curious way to begin a book about creativity, but I must start here. My central premise is we must first undo the damage of popular misconceptions about ideas and how they work, and in that undoing progress will naturally ensue.

The best place to start is to recognize that creativity, as a subject of study, is a modern invention. Ten thousand years ago people were too busy solving real problems in their lives to worry much about how to label those solutions, or what to call the people who made them. They also made art and music for their own pleasure and didn't worry much about what to call that either. They went and did it because they wanted to. Even the masters of the Renaissance, like Raphael and Donatello, and of the Enlightenment, like Locke and Descartes, didn't talk much about brainstorming exercises or ideation methods. This should make us suspicious about the modern obsession with studying creativity as a thing unto itself.

We can learn three simple rules from our ancestors in this regard:

1.   If there's something you want
      to do, you must simply go and
      do it.
2.   If you want to be better at
      something, do it more often.
3.   If you want to improve faster,
      ask someone who knows more
      than you to watch you and
      give their advice.

Perhaps this seems blindingly obvious, but you are overlooking the fact that right now as you read this you are breaking all of these rules. Currently you are merely reading. Reading is a wonderful way to learn, but it is still a kind of consumption, as while reading you are not creating anything. You won't really be working on your creative skills until you put this book down and go make something. With today's abundance of knowledge from websites and books, we forget that knowing something is not the same as doing something.

The word *create* is a verb. It's an action. Creativity is best thought of in the same way—it's something you can use while involved in an activity, like painting, writing, debating or dancing. If someone tells me they want to be more creative, I will immediately ask, "Creative in doing what?" which often gives them pause. Even if they're clever and say "I want to be more creative at thinking itself!" I will still direct them to a craft, perhaps writing or filmmaking, as they need a medium in order to develop the skills of improving how they think, creatively or otherwise.

Even more insidious than forgotten lessons from our ancestors is how we've burdened ourselves with a strange obsession for labeling things. Is this cool? Is this creative? Is this innovative? Instead of simply putting effort into the skill of making good things, or merely enjoying ourselves regardless of the quality of the outcome, we worry if it meets someone else's subjective approval. The word *creative* is often used to mean novel, a new idea or way of doing something. But in this very limited use of the word there is a big problem. A person ignorant of Western culture who has never seen a chocolate chip cookie will think it is very creative, while all of us in the West know this is a very old and traditional (yet very tasty) thing. Creativity as novelty is therefore always relative. What one person finds novel might be old news to someone else. This means worrying about what one person calls creative is often a wild goose chase in discerning their tastes, preferences and experiences.

It's far wiser to think about the effect you want an idea to have. If the goal is to make someone laugh, fix their car or increase the revenue of the widgets their company makes, that matters far more than how "creative" an idea is or is not. An idea can be very creative, interesting and inspiring and yet not solve a single problem for anyone. And the counterpoint is true as well. If you were deathly ill and needed medical care, you wouldn't argue with doctors on the creative merits of their approach. No one has ever said, "Stop this surgery! This will cure me, but it's not creative enough!" We all know in our real lives that creativity is rarely the most important thing, but when it comes to ideas we forget creativity is a means to an end, not often an end unto itself.

If there is a goal of some kind that you are after, something you want creativity to achieve for you, you should know what that is. It could simply be that you want to create something that pleases you. Perhaps you want to write a great play that changes people's minds on a subject you care about. It could be you want to create a billion-dollar company. Whatever it is, it's important to define it. Otherwise, you'll be chasing your subjective tail, and the subjective tails of others, running around like drunken philosophers endlessly debating the definition of every word instead of getting anything done.

A healthier perspective is that creativity is simply making interesting choices. If this is true, then creativity can be found just about anywhere—in small amounts, perhaps, but it's there nevertheless. There can even be creativity in how consumers, people who don't make anything, consume things. At a fast food restaurant watch how people choose to eat their hamburgers (with the left hand or right? What condiments do they use, or don't? How do they add them?). Or at work, watch how people sign their names or arrange their desks. If you are around children, watch them finger-paint and build worlds in *Minecraft* and you'll see effortless creation without them ever even thinking of the word. Even as bored adults, with lives defined by stressful morning commutes and boring daily routines, we make choices all day long, and in every one of those choices is the possibility to do something interesting.

Consider the decisions you made today. Did you go to work the usual way, or take a route without being sure where it would lead? When you dressed this morning, did you put on the boring socks and underwear, or the fun ones? Are you reading this book the normal way, or are you lying upside down and holding it above your head? We always have more freedom than we think, we just forget. We spend so much time trying to be efficient that doing anything interesting feels like a waste of time. And in this tendency is another misconception: creativity is rarely efficient. It always involves taking chances and trying things that might work but might not. The question then is: are we willing to spend time to be interesting, to think interesting thoughts and make interesting things?

We all have the power, but perhaps not the willingness.

I encourage you at this point to put on your creative socks, if you have any, before continuing this book. If you don't own any creative socks, take a pair of boring socks you never wear because of their unbearable ordinariness, perhaps they were a gift from a very dull third cousin who lives in the flat and distant lands of Boredomvania, and transform them. With a thick marker or pen write CREATIVE, or FUN, on each one. This is your first act of creative defiance: make something interesting out of something boring. Is this a transformational, world-changing idea? No. But it is possibly interesting, and that is the best first place to aim for. Many great ideas are really just interesting ones that were highly refined over time by a motivated mind.

If you don't like the very idea of this sock project because it seems silly to you, I say ha. Being silly often leads to having fun, and having fun means you are more likely to try new things. How do you expect to be more creative if you're not willing to try anything you haven't done before? Not willing to try makes you a victim of the status quo, the greatest killer of potential since the dawn of humanity.

Many books on creativity trivialize the subject by making it all about games and crafty projects, and it'd be fair to complain that with my sock project I am pushing you toward the same trap. However, I ask you to only make this complaint after you've enhanced your socks, not before. This is a good rule for new things, as we instinctively dismiss opportunities in life out of fear of being made uncomfortable, a feeling that comes with growth (which we claim to desire). Lastly, if your objection is the absurdity of having a book dictate that you be "creative" by forcing you to follow a "fun" instruction, I commend you for your sense of autonomy. For you I suggest using whatever label you wish, perhaps "oppressive pseudo-creative project," but good luck fitting that on your sock.

This chapter began with a question about where creativity comes from, and I gave you a mostly dishonest and silly answer. Here is a more serious one. We get the majority of our creative powers from our subconscious mind.[1] We all know that our nighttime dreams, where we experience wild stories and vivid images, are things we do not consciously choose. They feel like they are happening to us, right until we wake up and realize our own mind created the experience.

There is a similar set of cognitive powers, fueled by our subconscious, that give us ideas while we are awake. We

---

[1] Mihaly Csikszentmihalyi, *Creativity: Flow and the Psychology of Discovery and Invention* (New York: Harper Perennial, 2013).

[2] Daniel Schacter, *The Seven Sins of Memory: How*

have all had an experience when we were stuck on a problem and decided to stop. Then, hours later, perhaps while doing the laundry or going for a walk, surprise! Suddenly, as if out of nowhere, a solution surfaces in our mind. It feels magical and leads us to think that perhaps, yes, there are aliens from Saturn giving us these ideas. The truth is far simpler: your subconscious mind has been working on the problem for you. Our subconscious minds are better at making associations and connecting diverse ideas than our conscious minds are, which explains the wild, but sometimes insightful, experiences we have in our sleep. There are ways to help this part of your mind work for you, and we will get to them later in this book.

Despite what science tells us about our subconscious, there is a powerful romantic appeal of creativity having an external source, coming from a place, a spirit or a substance outside of us (perhaps even a book). It's attractive because if creativity is a product, or a possession, then it's something we can just go and purchase like a candy bar or a box of blueberry doughnuts. If this were true, we could escape the challenge of understanding ourselves and how our own individual minds work. Instead of hoping for magical desserts, we should simply become comfortable asking ourselves the following questions:

- In what situations do I feel most creative?
- How can I protect time each day to work on a creative project?
- What are the daily habits of creative people I admire?
- What attitudes do I have that help or hinder me?
- Why do I own so many boring socks?

These questions scare most people because they require us to think, and mostly we don't like to think (though we like to think that we do). Thinking takes time and requires effort, but I can promise you here, at the close of this opening chapter, that time and effort are required for anything interesting you wish to do with your creative powers. This has been and always will be true.

This book is divided into three parts. Each part has a series of short chapters, some only a page long. Some chapters explain a technique, while others explore, or debunk, a way of thinking. It's a short book by design because if I have written it well, you will soon want to work on something where you can apply your creativity, and the faster I get out of your way, the better. Huzzah! And Tally Ho!

2. HOW TO BEGIN

Imagine that you land on the friendly planet Walden in a nice little energy-efficient spaceship/house, with all your favorite people and favorite things. All around you, for the entirety of the world, are undiscovered lands. If your goal is to explore to find interesting things, will it matter which direction you go in first? Any choice you make for where to start will result in a discovery of some kind, even if it is finding an impenetrable radioactive swamp of industrial waste (much to Thoreau's dis-appointment) or, more likely, learning there is nothing but ordinary forest nearby. But that first discovery, whatever it is, good or bad, will inform you about where to explore next and possibly what to look for or avoid. You will have made the tremendous psychological leap from having zero knowledge to having a little knowledge.

The same is true about deciding where to start for creative work. To create means to make something new, at least for you, and to do something new is like going off of the map, or more precisely, deliberately choosing to go to a part of the map that is unknown. In this case it rarely matters where or how you start. Many people obsess with trying to start in a perfect way, but that's a good sign they have the wrong attitude. The primary goal when you're starting creative work is to explore, and to explore demands you do things where you are not sure of the outcome. There will be false starts, twists, turns and pivots. These should be welcomed as natural parts of the experience, rather than resisted as mistakes or failures.

Of course for some projects like baking a cake or building a shed you could choose to use a recipe or buy a blueprint, but the level of creativity involved would be less than if you invented your own. As a strict rule, the more ambitious the project the more explorations you are going to need before you find the path you seek. From your house in Walden it'd take more wanderings to find a beautiful waterfall than, say, a handful of dirt. Many people claim to have the desire for creating masterpieces born of their own minds, but in reality they only want to expend the effort required by a paint-by-numbers *Mona Lisa* replica kit. Passion doesn't mean much unless you can convert it into the energy to do the work. The grander the idea, the more work you'll need to do.

To help getting started it's common for makers of all kinds, from artists to engineers to filmmakers, to keep a journal. A journal is simply a private place to put ideas, notions, questions, observations or inspirations so you can refer to them later. You won't know when you scribble something down what it means yet or how it might be used, but by putting it down it exists in the world and not just in your mind. Some makers keep one journal for all of their thoughts and sketches, but once they commit to a specific project they create a new journal. You will have to experiment to see what works best for you (an experiment about how you prefer to experiment, if you will).

The act of preserving your ideas is critical because humans have terrible memories—so awful, in fact, that we don't notice how much we forget. For example, what did I say in the third paragraph of the first page? Since it's written down you can easily return to it whenever you like. But if it wasn't written down and you didn't remember it, it'd be gone forever.[2] Our attention spans are very short, which means we likely have very interesting ideas cross

---

[2] Daniel Schacter, *The Seven Sins of Memory: How the Mind Forgets and Remembers* (New York: Mariner Books, 2002).

our minds every day that, uncaptured, fade away forever.

It's a biological fact that in any moment you are awake there are ideas you are thinking about. Most are banal, but some are interesting and may have potential. Maybe during boring conference calls at work you invent new ways to pretend like you are listening while you're really scrolling through Facebook. Or when you watch a bad movie, you easily see changes to make that would turn it into a good one. These little thoughts are seeds that, if given a safe place to live, might grow into something wonderful. The problem for most people is these ideas have nowhere to live. They quickly enter their minds and then just as quickly disappear forever. A journal is the safe place they need. It can be on paper or a digital device, it could be a sketchpad or a voice recorder—it doesn't matter as long as it's something you keep with you and find comfortable enough to use habitually.

Regardless of the means you choose for capturing ideas, if you don't take seriously the thoughts that cross your mind, no one else will have the chance to either. You must learn to love your mind, to nurture it by feeding it quality ideas and thoughts, and give it time to prove what it can do.

Often ideas come to mind when we're involved in another activity, and it can feel like a burden to have to take out our journal to write down what might just be a random thought. But I know that if I don't write it down, I'll never get a second chance to evaluate it again. Despite my convenient hope that I'll remember it later without writing it down, I know, scientifically, that I'll likely forget it, and forget that I forgot it. For this reason I fuel my idea journal discipline by imagining forgotten ideas as being cursed for eternity, falling for all time into an endless pit of darkness, crying my name out into the void knowing I will never hear their sad screams. Don't let this happen to your precious thoughts. Instead, put your ideas down somewhere, anywhere. Once they exist in the world there's always a chance, however small, you can return to them.

It's only by keeping a journal that you will notice useful patterns. After two weeks you might realize you get more ideas in the evening, or first thing in the morning, or when you wake in the night after a dream. Maybe it's when you are stuck driving in traffic, or perhaps it's when you are on the treadmill at the gym. If you keep a journal and diligently scribble down your thoughts, you'll encourage the creative part of your brain to speak up more often and more clearly. Your subconscious mind will get more confident at sharing with you what it observes, and you'll get better at feeding your mind with works by others that inspire you.

Don't judge what you put into your journal. No one else will see it. You may be surprised by some of what you put down, but that should fascinate you: you are getting to know your creative instincts and your subconscious better than you ever have before. This relationship is one of the most important you will ever have.

If you're interested in a specific project, like writing a book or a business plan, have a section in the journal that's just for thoughts about that project. At first the ideas will be random and maybe not all that interesting, but over time you'll have a pile of them that can be worked into a simple outline. Now you're on your way, and when you sit down to start, you will not be working from scratch. You'll have a collection of thoughts and ideas to borrow from to fill your first blank pages.

3. ALL IDEAS ARE MADE OF OTHER IDEAS

A first principle of creativity is that ideas are everywhere. We are often so busy in our daily lives that we forget this fact. We spend most of our days struggling to get everything done and looking for ways to make our lives easier. But the first thing to learn if you want to make things yourself is to remember this little mantra: all ideas are made of other ideas.

Steve Jobs did not invent the computer. Mozart didn't invent the piano, and Rembrandt didn't invent paint. They built upon countless ideas developed by other people. Marie Curie, as brilliant as she was, didn't discover radioactivity in a flash of insight. Instead, she studied the history of chemistry and physics and conducted experiments to build on what was already known, which helped her become one of the only people in history to earn Nobel Prizes in both subjects. Even Einstein's famous formula $e=mc^2$ is mostly a combination of ideas developed by other scientists.[3] We have always borrowed, reused and stood on the shoulders of ideas that came before us, and we always will. This is a fundamental law of how ideas work.

It can be hard to see this fact because by the time we experience an idea, it is often manifested in a finished movie, book or painting. It seems complete on its own, and unless we are experts in that field, we don't see the countless references and inspirations that led to what we see. While Edison's light bulb and the Wright brothers' first plane are

---

[3] David Bodanis, *E=mc²: A Biography of the World's Most Famous Equation* (Berkley Publishing Group, 2001)

famous, the hundreds of ideas and inventions from other people that Edison and the Wrights reused rarely surface in history books.[4] We love to lionize creators, putting them on high pedestals so we can take more pleasure in looking up at them. Ordinary people find this sufficient. They take comfort in viewing creators as extraordinary, believing they have capacities beyond what mere mortals can achieve. But you are not reading this book to become ordinary. This means you must look more closely at things than other people do. You must be intensely curious about why things are the way they are to imagine the better ways they could become.

If you pick any song, invention or philosophy and walk backward through the history of its development, you'll

---

[4] Scott Berkun, *The Myths of Innovation* (Sebastopol, CA: O'Reilly Media, 2010). Yes, it's weird to footnote myself!

discover they are all recombinations of other ideas. Sometimes the grandest ideas, once you get past the romance you feel for them, are the easiest to dissect. What is an automobile? An engine + wheels. A telephone? Electricity and sound. Fettuccine Alfredo? Flat noodles and cheese sauce. On and on it goes. Even Shakespeare borrowed significantly from the stories of Sophocles (and Disney's *Lion King* is a retelling of Shakespeare's *Hamlet*), just as Aristotle incorporated thoughts from Plato. The act of creating an idea is always an act of bringing existing ideas together in some shape or form.

Of course, simply slamming two ideas together won't necessarily result in an interesting outcome. An engine that runs on cheese sauce would be a disaster (but perhaps a tasty one, although "engine cheese" would be a terrible name). Understanding the relationship between ideas helps your intuition decide which things might combine well. For example, an experienced musician knows certain chords work better with certain melodies. But to write a song, they will combine many ideas, in different ways, experimenting their way into creating something they desire. It takes time to develop the craft of combining ideas in interesting ways, but it can only begin when you see ideas for what they are.

Whenever you look at a painting, watch a film, eat a meal or even listen to a business lecture or sit in a meeting at work, ask yourself: what is the central idea? What ideas were combined to create this? And then ask yourself: if I rearrange these ideas, what creative possibilities can I make?

4. EIGHT (OR MORE) METHODS FOR FINDING IDEAS

Finding interesting ideas is not very hard. For example, I've often wondered why there isn't a car that runs on laughter, can teleport instantly to habitable planets in other galaxies, and exhausts only harmless lemon-scented fumes that cure cancer. Now that's an *idea*. Of course it's entirely improbable given what we know about science, but it's an idea nevertheless, isn't it? What we really want in the end are good ideas we can make into something in the world: perhaps a book, an organization or a transportation device. Coming up with ideas is one thing, but ideas are just abstractions. An idea for a great film or invention can take a few seconds to think of but require years or decades to build, if it turns out to be possible at all.

Yet many popular books on creativity center on the promise of methods for coming up with ideas. The technique of brainstorming itself is focused on the volume of ideas it can generate. There is nothing wrong with having a big pile of ideas. In fact, this is an essential part of starting a project. You are looking to explore a wide range of territory, but a big pile of ideas like my laughter-fueled car can leave a lot of work to do no matter how many great ideas you have. Never forget this fact. Finding good ideas is one thing. Developing them into finished works is another.

However, because the romance about finding ideas is so strong, it's easy to think: if I have two ways to find ideas, won't having ten ways make me five times as creative? The answer is no. Having 100 hammers won't make you a better carpenter. You'd be better served by having a small number of different hammers you are familiar with and can use in different situations.

To that aim, here are the eight methods for finding ideas I teach and recommend. Some are straightforward exercises, while others involve attitudes you will need to develop. There are no rules here. Try them and see if they help. If not, there are plenty of others. In all cases you will quickly realize that a central element to the value of all of these methods is persistence.

1. Scout

Back on planet Walden, instead of picking a direction to explore at random, you could ask where your friends have gone and what they saw. You could climb onto your roof to get a better perspective of the entire landscape. For whatever kind of ideas you want to find, there is always a way to scout, or study, to learn more before you even begin. Having a map can help you decide which direction will be best.

Every kind of problem has a history of people who tried to solve it before. If you learn from what they did and why, you'll discover insightful questions you didn't even think to ask. People are often surprised to learn that the Wright brothers studied birds and how they flew. They exhausted the history of human ideas and scouted into the natural world, as did Leonardo da Vinci, to find models and methods they could reuse.

When you scout well, you'll find techniques and approaches that have been forgotten but are still useful today. For example, Alex Osborn's 1953 book *Applied Imagination* is a far better explanation of brainstorming, a term he coined, than what's practiced in the working world decades later. The greatest fuel for combining ideas might just be to take ideas from two different generations, cultures or places that haven't been used together before. Many breakthroughs occur when someone wanders from one field into another, as they're willing to try things, motivated by insight or ignorance, that others are not. Fusion cooking, where food traditions from two different parts of the world are combined, is an excellent example of what's possible if you recognize that the boundaries between groups of ideas are often arbitrary. But you can't make this recognition without some awareness of what kinds of food already exist.

Even late into a project, when you are stuck and don't feel like creating, you can still use scouting and study to your advantage. Read a biography about a hero in your field. Watch a documentary about how something you use every day was made. There are always ways to fuel your future creativity even if you don't feel like creating anything right now. A walk through an art museum or a hike on a scenic trail can allow your mind to interact with ideas, shapes and feelings, which might just be combinable with something you are working on. Your subconscious is always working in the background, making connections and insights for you. While strolling through town or across a hillside might seem like leisure to others, you know ideas are made from other ideas, and there will be more going on in your mind than people assume.

With your journal in hand, you can make notes from what you observe. Writing in your journal is a mini-creation, your own notes based on someone else's work. In that act of creating by responding to something else, you might discover a way through whatever has been blocking you.

2. Combine or Divide

If all ideas are made of other ideas, then the challenge is to combine them in interesting ways. Cooking is a good analogy for creativity: a chef's talent is in their ability to bring ingredients together to create something new. Even the most brilliant chefs do not make towering cheese soufflés or perfect lobster risotto through concentration alone. They must also use excellent ingredients and techniques developed by other people. They choose them carefully and then combine, refine and develop them into delicious dishes. A good chef can also break one item down into many. If you give them a whole chicken, they can divide it into its component parts, each of which can be used in different ways to make different dishes. The same is true for ideas of all kinds. You can always break an idea down into smaller ones, or combine small ones together into larger ones.

With any set of ideas you can:

- Bring two or more ideas together
- Divide an idea into smaller ones
- Use the ideas in a different order
- Get rid of, or add, an idea

Here's an example. Quickly pick two things in front of you, say this book and your smelly dog Rupert. Now imagine different ways to divide them and different ways to combine those parts—make sure your creative socks are on first. Or if you wish, add a third idea into the mix. If you're stuck, here are some ideas I came up with:

- A book about Rupert
- A smelly book
- A book chapter about Rupert's creativity
- A clone of Rupert made entirely out of engine cheese
- A book about a smelly clone of Rupert made entirely out of low fat engine cheese

If you withhold judgment about any particular combination until later, you can quickly generate dozens of ideas. While many of these combinations might be terrible, weird, strange or even offensive, they're certainly interesting. Adding a fourth element, say a gallon of black coffee, might yield even more interesting combinations (a book about a smelly clone of Rupert made of engine cheese that gives you a caffeine high when you read it).

Another approach to finding interesting combinations is called a mind map. On a large piece of paper write your main goal, subject or idea down in the center and circle it. Then think of an attribute, or an idea, related to the main one and write it down, drawing a line back to the main idea. Then think of another and another, connecting each one to any previous idea that seems most related. Keep drawing lines and making associations. Soon you'll have a page full of circles and lines capturing different ways to think about your main thought.

Don't worry about accuracy or even coherency while you do this. You simply want to let the associative part of your mind, the part that's good at finding connections between different things, to have its way for a while. Mind maps are helpful because they are nonlinear and nonlogical. They allow you to express your thoughts in shapes and curves, rather than in neat columns and straight lines.

Once you run out of steam, the value of the map becomes clearer. You can pick any two items you wrote down and combine them, asking: "What could this be?" Here's an example mindmap by Frank Chimero about Chuck Norris.[5]

---

[5] Modified with permission from Chimero's essay How To Have An Idea http://www.frankchimero.com/writing/how-to-have-an-idea.

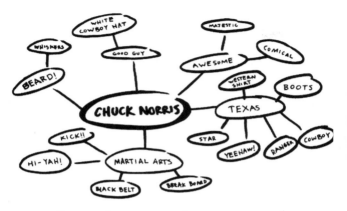

Over time, creative masters learn combinations or patterns that can be used again and again to develop new ideas or modify old ones. They find exercises, like mind maps, that help them explore what's in their mind.

In any particular craft there are combinations, and types of combinations, that become familiar because they tend to work well. There are good reasons many famous films have a likable underdog who overcomes tough challenges. It's no surprise that most cuisines have some kind of bread stuffed with tasty fillings. It takes dedication to learn these patterns in any field, and to develop ways to transcend them into being more than just clichés. Over time your instincts for which combinations to try first, or to try to obtain a specific quality, will improve.

3. Kill False Constraints

We're afraid. We're afraid of the dark, of our parents and what our parents do in the dark. Our powerful reptilian brains do their best to keep us from thinking about things we fear or don't understand. This is good for survival, but bad for creativity. We shut down the pursuit of many combinations because of predictions we make about the result. Will this idea offend Bob? Will I be embarrassed if I say this out loud? We're scared to think certain thoughts or even to write them down.

Making a list of the constraints, both practical and psychological, about a project can reveal limitations you are creating that don't need to exist (fear is a kind of imagination, after all). If you can remove a false constraint, new possibilities, and combinations, will instantly be revealed. Even if a constraint is real—perhaps you have a tiny budget—putting it aside for a time can allow more possible combinations to try. After you have some promising ideas, bring the constraint back. You may discover with a specific good idea in hand you are motivated to overcome the constraint and find possibilities you wouldn't have tried to find before.

Constraints can be helpful. It's easy to think the fewer you have the better, but that's rarely true. They focus your attention and force you to think, rather that simply spending resources. Adding challenging constraints, for a time, can let you see a problem in a new way, leading to ideas that are valuable even when the constraint is removed.

4. Play the Opposite Game (It's Good to Be Bad)

Normally people assume the goal is to find good ideas, but this creates psychological pressure. The desire to perform well intensifies certain fears we have about being judged or feeling inadequate. A fantastic technique to escape these traps is to take ten minutes to deliberately find terrible ideas. I call this the opposite game. It works best with groups of people but can also be used solo.

For example, if your real goal was to invent a better mobile phone case, instead switch to the goal of inventing the most terrible one ever created. By framing the goal this way, we lower our psychological stakes. Instead of feeling pressure, we feel free and encouraged to have fun. And then combining these "bad" ideas makes for ideas that are increasingly terrible, and often quite funny.

A session like this might generate terrible ideas like:

- It weighs 575 lbs
- It only comes in blinking neon pink.
- It smells like rotting cheese
- It drains your battery four times as fast (to power the blinking neon light)
- It gives you tuberculosis (and makes your breath smell worse every time you speak into the phone)

Once the pace of finding new ideas and combinations slows, you know it's time to stop. If you set the right tone, morale will be high. People will have shared laughter and truly collaborated by building new ideas based on ideas they heard. This, on its own, is a sizable achievement. Many creativity exercises fail because they never get the group of people in the room to start to trust and connect with each other.

There is a final, possibly more directly productive, bonus step. Go through the list of "bad" ideas and, with the group, try to invert each one back into a good idea.

Good ideas (by inverting bad ones):

- It weighs almost nothing.
- It comes in any color a customer wants.
- It smells like your favorite perfume.
- It gives extra battery life.
- It protects you from, and detects, germs in the air (and freshens your breath).

Finding good ideas is always easier after inventing some terrible ones first. Your creative energies are already flowing, you've had some fun, and if you're working with other people, you've established some trust in each other from all the laughs and ideas you created together.

5. Switch Modes

There are many ways to express a thought. You can sketch, write, talk or even sing. If you switch the way you're expressing the idea, or the mode, different kinds of ideas, or improvements to the idea, will be easier to find. There's an old joke about trying to explain a notion through an interpretive dance. Usually this is meant to mock that we can go too far in abstracting away from what we're trying to express, when a more direct method will do. However, there is a truth in it too, at least for the interpretive dancer. Even a failed attempt to convey an idea will force you to think differently, and that might just be enough for you to see a new path. Like a game of charades, realizing the current approach you are taking isn't working might just be the motivation you need to seek and find a better one.

Here are some easy ways to switch modes:

- Write with your opposite hand
- Look at your work upside down, from ten feet away or while standing on top of it Jackson Pollock style
- Put sunglasses on (make the work black and white)
- Represent your project as a cartoon, a short film or... an interpretive dance
- Try to explain your project to someone who knows nothing about it, perhaps a child, a neighbor or a friend you know will ask challenging questions

Of course these are all experiments. You can't be sure which one will yield the new perspective you desire. But even the slightest new insight can provide the leverage needed for a breakthrough.

6. Change the Environment

Creativity is personal. We are all unique, and it's in understanding how we are different that gives us greater potential to find interesting ideas. This means you must spend time asking yourself questions like:

- When do ideas come easiest to me?
- Is it when I am alone or with friends?
- Is it in busy places like bars and coffee shops, or quiet ones like a library?
- Are there times of the day when I'm most relaxed and thinking freely is easier?

Changing the environment you are in will likely change the way you feel and think. Even if you've learned your own patterns for productivity, changing them for a day or an hour will give you a different kind of energy to work with. You might discover your preferences have changed. Or you'll hate the new environment so much that when you return to your preferred one you'll feel a boost of comfort and motivation.

7. Find a Partner

Many people are most productive when they're with people whose company they enjoy. Partnering on a project, or even being around other creative people who are working on solo projects, can have a stimulating effect. It also gives you a person to lean on who will understand your situation when things go sour. It should not be a surprise how many great works in history were made by people working in pairs or small groups: Paul McCartney and John Lennon, Charles and Ray Eames, and Gilbert and Sullivan. Some of these relationships were contentious, but it was a productive tension that pushed both parties to do better work.[6]

But remember that everyone is different. You might work best on your own, or with only a certain kind of partnership. Perhaps what you need most is a mentor, or a mentee. Maybe you just need someone who will give you honest feedback. For every project, it's possible you will need a different combination of relationships with other people to achieve what you want.

8. Lock Yourself in a Closet

When someone tells me they're stuck and can't find any ideas at all, I ask if they have ever been locked in a closet. I

---

[6] The concept of creative abrasion, created by Jerry Hirshberg, is defined as a useful tension between teammates where they challenge each other to do their best work. See Jerry Hirshberg, *The Creative Priority* (New York: Harper Collins, 1999).

admit this is a strange thing to ask someone, but it's surprising to learn how many people have locked their siblings in all sorts of terrible places, including closets. Anyway, I ask this question not to study fraternal social disorders but because anyone locked in a closet for a sufficient amount of time will become very creative in trying to find ways to get out. It's pure biology. When you are stuck in a place you don't want to be in, all sorts of possibilities, some more creative and desperate than others, come to mind, and they come with the courage to try them out. It's a reminder of how easily we forget what we are capable of at any time.

Now of course it'd be silly to lock yourself in a closet every time you wanted to compose a song or bake a cake, but some famous creators, including authors Po Bronson and Annie Dillard, have done it. Some professionals ask to be locked in hotel rooms to meet deadlines, or retreat to a cabin in the woods with no internet or electricity. It can be a kind of ritual (of their environment) for some people in that they rely on having a place where there are few distractions and they can find just the right balance of "comfortable enough but not too comfortable" to be productive. Some artists have very carefully constructed their studios to create the perfect atmosphere for themselves, but this is extremely personal. If you took any two of these people and made them work in each other's workspaces, the results would likely be disastrous. So don't look at any of your hero's habits as the answer, but as merely an experiment to consider trying.[7]

Personally, I like to believe I have enough self-discipline that I don't need to be physically trapped in small,

---

[7] See Mason Currey, *Daily Rituals: How Artists Work* (New York: Alfred A. Knopf, 2013).

unpleasant spaces to achieve ambitious things. However, I do use the *idea* of it to help me. Sometimes when I don't want to work, or don't feel creative, I close my eyes and imagine being locked in a closet. I consider how, if that happened, I'd rediscover my primal powers of creativity that I forgot I had. Just the thought of it often changes my attitude. The blank page doesn't seem anywhere near as tough as scratching my fingers raw from reaching underneath the closet door, with my stomach aching for a morsel of food, my soiled jeans sticking to my bony thighs, my throat burning from days of unanswered screams... Okay, perhaps that's more than you need to know about the dark visions at work in my mind. The lesson is that real or imagined states of going without can be potent motivation.

9. Meta-Methods

If all ideas are made of other ideas, what does that mean for this chapter? Any of the methods above can be combined in different ways, and each one has many creative variations to try. You may have realized that being locked in a closet is just an extreme version of changing your environment, which suggests there are other possibilities. Maybe a picnic at a park with a friend, combined with the inversion game, is what you need. There are always new experiments to try, and since we are changing all the time, we can never quite predict when an old method will fail us, or when a new one will save the day.

5. THE DANCE OF THE POSSIBLE

All projects are a dance between two forces, expanding to consider more ideas and shrinking to narrow things down enough to finish. For example, in the course of writing a book, authors go through many phases of this dance, at levels both large and small. Even something as simple as deciding the title of a book involves this dance. Many writers generate lists of possible titles, exploring all sorts of combinations and directions, including soliciting suggestions from friends and fans. But then eventually they must decide on a single title, casting all of the other choices aside. If they don't spend enough time exploring possibilities, the odds of having a good title are lower. But if they spend too much time exploring, they won't have enough time to solve other important problems.

I call this a dance because unlike the diagrams I'm about to show you, it's an intuitive process rather than a logical one. There is no algorithm you can use to be certain you've spent the right amount of time exploring. This is similar to asking questions like: how many wines should you sample before buying an entire bottle? Even if the first one is delicious, might the next one be even better? How good is good enough? What if instead of wine, the decision is buying a house? Or finding a spouse? The more time you use to explore each possible option, the longer it takes to get anything done. But if you don't spend enough time exploring alternatives, you probably won't like the results. Since any creative project consists of hundreds of choices, large and small, you are guaranteed to do a lot of dancing.

As I mentioned, I have some diagrams to share with you. While diagrams can be enlightening, consume them carefully. In trying to convey one concept, diagrams often unintentionally let people assume that no other concepts apply. Diagrams, like maps, work because of what they omit, leaving things out to help make one point clear. Even worse, some diagrams make you feel like you've learned something, but teach nothing because they've omitted important details. For example, take this diagram:

It's wonderfully simple until you sit your pre-amazing body down in a chair and try to apply what you learned from the diagram. It's good advice to consume all diagrams with caution. Too often they maddeningly skip right past all of the hard parts, pretending that they don't exist at all.

With that warning in place, here's a diagram for the first part of the dance. In any creative act, from picking where to go on vacation to deciding on the plot for your screenplay, the shape looks like this:

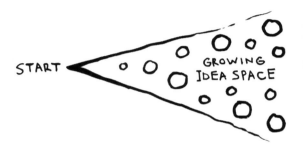

As you come up with ideas, and pull the best ones from your journal, the space of possibilities for what the project can be grows. And if you're good at seeing combinations, and add them as you should, it grows fast. If you're working with other people who collaborate well, it grows even faster.

The fancy word for this is *divergence*. Most of what people think of as creative work is divergent in that the goal is to come up with as many interesting ideas as possible, especially ideas that are different from each other. Diverging is often great fun. It's exhilarating. Anything can be considered, including wonderfully bold but impractical ideas. It's important to always play with a few impractical notions, as some will turn out, after you play with them awhile, to be more possible than you first assumed.

In the end the only projects the world will ever see are the ones that get finished. And to finish something means it has to converge all the way down to a singular (or maximally convergent) work. That may happen after a week of effort or a decade, depending on how ambitious the project is, and how many different alternatives you choose to explore before making each decision.

Therefore, the second half of the dance is as important as the first. With each decision that gets made the number of possibilities for what the work will be shrinks, which looks like this:

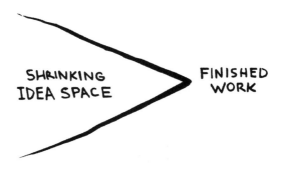

SHRINKING IDEA SPACE

FINISHED WORK

Here's an example that might help the entire dance make better sense. Imagine you have just finished writing a novel about life on the planet Walden. If you did it like many authors do, you successfully wrote one draft, obtained useful feedback from wise colleagues, wrote a second draft, obtained more precise feedback and then wrote a final version. In terms of diverging and converging, it would look something like this:

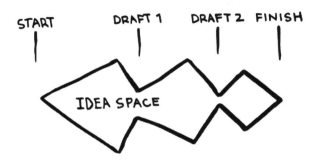

Looking back on a finished project, you might think the time spent exploring ideas that didn't get used was wasted. It's easy to believe you should have known from the beginning which ideas would work best and which wouldn't. This is an illusion. Creativity is exploration. You are going into the unknown on purpose. You can only learn about ideas as you develop them, and there's no reliable predictor of which ones will pay off and which ones won't. Certainly the more conservative you are in the ideas you pick, the more predictable the process will be, but by being more conservative you are likely being less creative and will discover fewer insights. Arguably the more creations you make the better your intuition gets, but you won't find any successful creator, even the legends, who gets it right all the time.

People obsessed with efficiency have a hard time accepting this truth. They would also have a very hard time being at sea with Magellan, working with Edison in his lab or with Frida Kahlo in her art studio. They'd be stunned to see the "waste" of prototypes and sketches, and mystified by how many days Magellan had to spend at sea without discovering a single thing. Discovery is never efficient.

The fantasy is that there could be a person so brilliant that their idea space for a project would look like this:

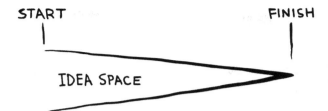

START

FINISH

IDEA SPACE

The only reason to expect a shape like this is if you were doing a project very much like ones you'd done before, say, cooking macaroni and cheese from a box for the 500th time. But you wouldn't call your achievement a creative one (Yes, you did *make* dinner for someone, but that's not as creative as inventing a new kind of meal to serve). If you like certainty, pick projects more like making macaroni and cheese. If you have more ambition, accept that you will be doing lots of inefficient dances.

Another possible explanation for the diagram above is that you had a complete and precise vision in your mind for all the details of the thing you wanted to create. And that your mastery of craft was so supreme that all you needed to do was put your vision down in confident strokes onto paper or a canvas of some kind. This is possible but so unlikely that you should pretend I never told you it was possible at all. Many legends exist of writers or musicians creating an entire book or a dozen songs over a weekend, but if you do some digging you'll find they're almost always exaggerations. Yes, Ray Bradbury did write 25,000 words of *Fahrenheit 451* in just a few days. But what's often not told about that amazing burst of productivity is that he later revised the book several times over the course of a year, expanding its length and heavily editing it, before it reached its final published form. In every legendary story of bursts of creativity there is a dance somewhere if you look carefully.

I recommend looking for more representative stories, like how J.K. Rowling filled five pages in a notebook of invented words starting with q before she settled on Quidditch.[8] Or that Hemingway wrote 47 different versions of the ending of his famous novel *A Farewell To Arms*.[9] Why did Rowling and Hemingway need to do this? We'd think someone with their talents would have projects that look like the last diagram above, nearly a straight line without much "waste." Hemingway didn't try 47 different versions of every section of the book of course (if you're not fond of his mini-

---

[8] "J. K. Rowling on *The Diane Rehm Show*," October 20, 1999, http://www.accio-quote.org/articles/1999/1299-wamu-rehm.htm.

[9] Julie Bosman, "To Use and Use Not," The *New York Times*, July 4, 2012, http://www.nytimes.com/2012/07/05/books/a-farewell-to-arms-with-hemingways-alternate-endings.html.

malist style you might wish that he had), and Rowling didn't fill pages in a notebook before deciding on every single word she wrote. The lesson to learn from these examples is to prioritize our dancing. We have to pick which handful of decisions are worth spending time doing grand explorations, and which ones to make quickly and cleanly.

This dance of possibilities is like life in many ways. We are never entirely sure we've made the "best" choices about careers, partners or where we live. Is there a better option out there? How can we be sure there isn't? And sometimes in life it is not our choice to keep dancing. Sometimes it's a client, or a boss, or a spouse who tells us we must revise and rethink a task we believe is already finished. Or that we must hurry up on a decision we think is worthy of more time. Sometimes we learn in revising our work that they were right, but sometimes even after more exploring we merely confirm the dance was done all along.

Knowing about this dance won't directly help you come up with better ideas. It also won't, on its own, help you make better decisions. But being familiar with the feel of the dance, and finding ways to embrace and enjoy it, will serve you well, as you will spend much of your time dancing as you work.

6. HOW TO DEVELOP A CONCEPT

The more I think about creative thinking, the more I believe it's really just *thinking*. The extra word isn't necessary. When I break down what any creative person does into the smallest pieces, it's just a series of thoughts and decisions. The word *think* itself means

to have a particular opinion, belief or idea about someone or something.

If to think means to be in possession of an idea, better thinkers have more ideas to work with. They also have a better sense for which ideas apply to which situations. Taking the word *creative* out of the whole mess simplifies things dramatically. It also reveals that if someone doesn't have enough working brain cells for regular thinking, they're probably not going to do all that well at the creative kind either.

Problem-solving is perhaps my favorite term of all, if I have to use one. Problem-solving implies there is a specific target, a problem, to guide our thinking. The chosen problem might be to paint an inspiring mural for the town square or simply fix a leaky kitchen faucet. It could also be to invent a new kind of faucet that never leaks. Any dream or situation can be described as a problem to be solved, and the more ambitiously you define the problem, the more ambitious the kinds of thoughts are that you're going to need to solve it.

If you think of the dance of possibilities itself as a problem to solve, there's at least one straightforward approach. Since you can't explore every possibility, the challenge, especially early in a project, is to explore the ones that will teach you the most. This usually means picking two or three ideas, or concepts, you think are promising but are very different from each other. And for each one take time, perhaps an hour or a day, to flesh out the idea as if it were the only one you had. Those investments of effort will teach you much about all of the other ideas and help you decide what the next dance step should be.

Developing ideas is easier if you succeed in generating a big list of ideas to work from. Go through that list and group ideas with similar traits. Even if you have 100 ideas, you can group them into a few rough piles. If your project is to write a novel, you could group your ideas by genre or by theme. If the project is to start a company, you could group your ideas by type of product or the business model you'd use. Or in my example above of inventing a new type of faucet, the groups would be based on different techniques for redesigning the faucet. You're effectively dividing up the space of all ideas into groups you can more easily work with.

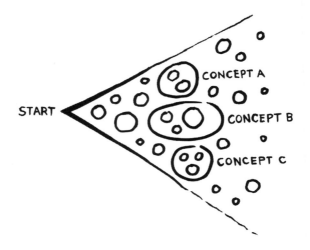

For each interesting concept you have, spend time thinking about the next level of detail. Ask the question: if I chose this concept, what is the first series of questions I'd have to answer to make it real? When we first come up with an idea it's often just a sentence or a thought. To make it into a concept requires fleshing the idea out, perhaps into a sketch, a draft or even building a rough prototype. In some cases you might just have a list of questions to research.

As an example, here's what I did for the "ultra-deluxe-mega-neverleak faucet" project. After making a big list of possible ideas, I grouped them and realized they were all variations on three different concepts: a) change the material, b) improve the washer (which warps as it ages and often causes leaks) or c) improve the faucet head. For each one I made a quick sketch to help me see what one possibility of the concept might be like.

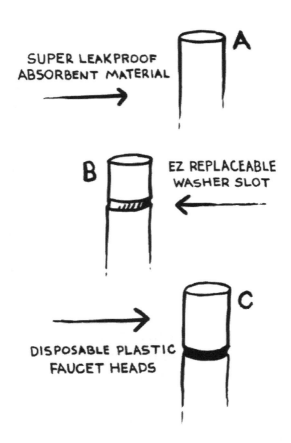

SUPER LEAKPROOF
ABSORBENT MATERIAL →

A

B

EZ REPLACEABLE
WASHER SLOT ←

→

DISPOSABLE PLASTIC
FAUCET HEADS

C

Since I didn't follow my own advice from previous chapters, and did exactly zero scouting, these ideas are likely impractical, misguided or impossible to build. But even so, with these first concepts in hand I can start asking better questions. For example, in concept A I'm assuming there exists a better material for faucets that attracts droplets of water, absorbing them back inside before they hit the sink and make that irritating "plop" sound. Does such a substance exist? Where would I find it? What skills would I need to invent it myself? And in each question there is more scouting to do to find the answer.

I could also show the concepts to a plumber and listen to their feedback. Or I could go take a kitchen faucet apart and understand better how it works. I'd likely realize, with some actual real world information, that concept C was entirely useless and abandon it. And then if I applied some of the idea generation methods from earlier in this book I'd quickly find new ideas for variations. A would become A1, A2, A3 and A4. B would become B1, B2, B3 and

B4. I'd probably also have more knowledge and could come up with concepts D and E. [10]

Suddenly J.K. Rowling's five notebook pages don't seem like so many. For even a simple problem, there are a tremendous number of ways to consider solving it. Developing an idea into a concept is simply a matter of adding the next level of detail to each promising option, which allows you to ask the next level of detailed questions. Some of the answers you find will clarify that the idea can't work, and you'll abandon that

---

[10] One idea that came to mind during these explorations was why have a faucet at all? Why not have a *Star Trek*-style replicator that would instantly fill containers I put in my sink with the right volume of water? While this is impossible given the limits of modern science, it does question the assumptions of faucets. Is there a better way to fill containers or provide water for the tasks commonly performed in a sink? Or could those tasks be performed without water at all but with some other new invention?

path, helping you on the dance of possibilities. Others will reveal new paths to consider, and the idea space will get wider, if you decide they're worthy of more of your time.

7. WHAT IS GOOD?

Is the automobile a good idea, considering the traffic and pollution it creates? Is Bob Dylan a good singer, given the raspiness of his voice? Is it good to start a chapter by asking a series of questions that I probably won't get around to answering? On the surface we use the word *good* as if it has a singular, universal meaning, but when applied to any specific choice in the world we can find intelligent people who disagree about how good it is or is not. Even Plato and Aristotle argued about what the word means and never came up with an answer good enough to satisfy everyone.

I share this with you because you will often ask yourself, about things you are making, "Is this good?" All of the explorations you do in different drafts and prototypes are eventually evaluated on your sense of goodness. And you will, no matter how talented you are, have your finished works challenged and called not-so-good names. *Good* is surprisingly subjective, and the more creative the domain you work in, the more subjective it is.

The ambiguity of what is good is an unavoidable part of the creative experience, and you should not fear it. Every time your notion of good is challenged, if you can avoid taking it personally, you will grow. Either you'll discover you need to better explain the merits of your work, or that your work isn't as good as you assumed.[11] In all cases you'll see your creations from more points of view, and you'll grow from the experience. What does a master do for their pupil other than

---

[11] Scott Berkun, "How To Pitch an Idea", http://scottberkun.com/essays/38-how-to-pitch-an-idea/.

help them understand what good can mean and how to achieve it?

The ability to see an idea, or a thing, from many different perspectives is among the greatest assets a thinking person can have. Of course you don't have to agree with someone else's perspective, but you owe it to yourself to try to see what they do. They may see something important you've never noticed before, however small, that can improve what you're making or what you make in the future.

What is good is relative to the type of thing you are creating. If you're an engineer building an eight-lane highway drawbridge to cross a dangerous river, there are functional definitions of good, like not opening at random times during rush hour, that are less subjective. For most works there is a moral goodness of not letting what you make harm anyone[12]. But for more creative projects, what we mean by good varies widely. For example, you could decide you want to make a horror film about what happens to ideas that aren't written down in their creator's journals. Or you could choose to create a screwball comedy about a cult of people who think way too much about how to be more creative. The nature of these two projects is so different in style that what would be good for one project, say the tense orchestral score for the horror film, would be bad for the other, and vice versa.

Therefore, it's wise to list the goals of a project. How will you know if you've succeeded at your idea? What will the

---

[12] Creators are notorious for letting their egos blind them from how their "wonderful" creations can be used for evil by those motivated by greed, selfishness or tyranny. Being creative doesn't necessarily mean you are moral or that your creations are good for the world.

person who sees, reads or consumes it feel if you've made it well? If you never clearly define what good means for a project, you will have a hard time knowing what to aim for or when you've hit your mark. And if you as the maker aren't sure what good means for a project, odds are whoever consumes your work won't either. Of course, you could do a dance of possibilities with your goals, deliberately exploring for exploring's sake, planning to decide what the project is only afterward. That playful freedom might lead to a great discovery, or might be a wild exploration that doesn't yield many rewards. There is no way to know for sure, and you'll have to learn which approach suits you best.

The variability of goodness applies even to our own perceptions. Our moods and assumptions change in every moment. A painting you loved years ago might not hold up very well when you see it again (as your tastes, or eyesight, may have changed). Sometimes you'll think an idea you just came up with is brilliant, only to realize, the next day, that you missed something important and that the idea is useless. The good news is that the opposite can happen too, if we are willing to keep ideas around us long enough for it to happen.

It's a well-known story in creativity books, but the invention of the Post-it note sheds a useful light on the subjective challenges of goodness. Art Fry was an engineer at 3M, working on a prototype for a new kind of super strong glue. The prototype was a failure: the glue he made turned out to be very weak, too weak to use to glue anything together. Instead of throwing it away, he kept it. In a sense he asked himself the question: "What is this good for?" He knew it certainly wasn't good for the problem it was intended for, but that didn't mean it wasn't good for *something*.

Every so often he would take the glue out again and think about what problem it could solve. For years he tried different things, and none of them worked. But he kept trying. Many of us would have given up and moved on, and with good reason. Few of his coworkers thought anything would come of it. Silver persisted, not entirely sure he was right but willing to keep asking the question.

Eventually a coworker named Spencer Silver tried to use this weak glue to place notes on sheets of choir music. It worked well, and they made more advanced prototypes. After a few more years of persistence to perfect the idea as a product, the Post-it note was born.

This story is often told in creativity books, but often to teach misleading lessons about unexpected results. I'm sharing with you because it expresses how variable goodness is, and also demonstrates habits many creative people naturally develop.

- **Keep a scrap pile**. If you are ambitious you will have many projects that don't turn out as you hoped. Don't throw them away. Keep them together in a box or on a shelf, and every now and then take them out again. Ask for each one: what is this good for? Do I see a new path to make it better, or can I strip it for parts and take this one paragraph or melody and combine it with something else? I don't know a single productive creative person who doesn't have a scrap pile of unfinished projects at different states of completion. This is not waste, but a precious archive of projects that might need to breathe, or of spare parts that may be perfect for other projects.

- **Use project scrapbooks or boxes**. Choreographer Twyla Tharp, in her excellent book *The Creative Habit*, describes how when she starts a project she creates a place for all the tidbits of inspiration, scraps of ideas or articles she thinks might be related to the idea she has in mind. Much like how you should keep a journal that you build over time, a project box lets you capture little pieces of the puzzle.

- **Postpone final judgments.** We can't predict what insights we'll have tomorrow. Silver trusted his instinct that his "bad glue" might have value he couldn't see yet. The only way to test that instinct in yourself is to keep some things around. Many won't turn out to be useful, but for the ones that will, there is no other way you can discover their value. Some movies and books are poorly received when they're released but become popular decades later. Others are big hits at first but fade over time. What is good? The answer depends on what your goals are and what problems you choose to solve.

8. WHY YOU SHOULD (LEARN TO) IMPROVISE

Many years ago, on a dare, I took a class in improvisation. I was surprised how much the class helped me experience daily life. It made me a better thinker, teacher and person in surprising ways. Recently I decided to take an improv class a second time, and again I was surprised! And surprised at how much I was surprised. I'd forgotten how much I'd forgotten, which, as noted earlier in this book, is a normal consequence of confronting the great limitations of human memory. Among the many things I learned, or relearned, is my conviction that anyone interested in working with ideas should take a full course in improvisational thinking.

Here are some wrong assumptions about improv classes:

- **It's not about being funny**. When I mention improv class to most people, they're instantly terrified. They assume the class consists of being thrown on a big dark stage where someone yells at them every few seconds to do something funny. The reality is the class is mostly playing games, simple ones, like saying sentences where you alternate words with someone else. The games get harder as the classes go on, but you're often told to avoid trying to be funny. Instead, the goal is to pay attention and to commit fully to whatever you're doing. If everyone does a few simple things well, the result is always interesting, and often comedic, but it's not a straight line.
- **You don't have to be a natural performer**. In the class you quickly learn that improv (and most drama)

depends on the commitment of actors to the scene they're in. Being "good" at improv is not a talent in a conventional sense, but more of a capacity for paying attention. Enthusiasm, concentration and willingness matter more than anything else, and anyone can choose to provide these three things.

- **It's not hard to learn**. Both times I've taken the class I've been amazed at what happens when you convince a bunch of ordinary strangers to faithfully follow the rules of the games. The rules are brilliant: they let magic emerge from the collective tensions and connections between human beings.

Here is what I learned:

- **I'd forgotten how to play**. The games played in improv might bore a typical eight-year-old, but for adults they're wonderful. Someone says, "Be an angry fish" and everyone says, "I'm an angry fish!" and you have a room full of professional men and women instantly running around acting like a bunch of happy children pretending to be an imaginary thing. The rules for the games are simple but depend on commitment. And I've rediscovered what children know: when I jump in all the way I'm surprised by what I can do. So much of adult life is doing things by half, or pretending to care when we know we don't. By rule, there is no half-assing in improv class. Whatever you are supposed to be right now, be it all the way.

- **Life is less stressful**. Now when I'm in challenging situations in life, a stressful meeting or getting lost in a strange city, I recall something ridiculous I was forced to do in improv class, like miming my way through the world championship of dishwashing, and by comparison the life situation suddenly seems easier. I'm more relaxed as a person from taking improv class. Fewer things cause me stress, as I've been in far crazier psychological situations each week while in class.

- **Questions and saying "No" are deadly**. The saying "Yes, and..." is the most well known of the basic rules of improvisation. Simply put, the only response you're ever allowed to have to anything that happens in class is to say "Yes, and..." to it. You have to accept whatever just happened, however bizarre, and build on it. The games in improv clarify how often, especially during divergent creative tasks, confrontational questions slow things down. It's a bad habit many of us have in life, asking dozens of pessimistic questions before we are willing to consider, much less try, anything new. The rule doesn't mean you have to do what others tell you, but that you have to find creative ways to build on the energy of whatever they've offered, and offer it back to them to build on in return. "What is this good for?" is one kind of question that stays in the spirt of "Yes, and...".

- **Improvisation is everywhere**. Every conversation in life is an act of improvisation: no one gives you a script for the day when you wake up. We don't often think of life this way, but every moment is a chance to observe and engage with the world in a new way. Improv helps me pay attention, proper attention, to all the situations I didn't realize I could influence. If we are curious about life, and learn how to grant open-minded attention to any moment, then discovery is possible almost anywhere and at any time.

- **Doing > thinking**. As I've offered earlier in this book, creativity is best thought of as an action. Life is experience, and reading about other people's experiences, as powerful as it can be depending on the writing, is still a shadow of having the experience yourself. Merely reading about improvisation, creativity or anything else of importance robs you of what you're seeking. Put yourself in the middle of things, something improv class makes natural and fun for every participant.

There are of course other ways to put yourself in situations that challenge how you think and feel. Going to a play, to an art museum or even on a hike in the woods can stimulate you and give rise to new thoughts. But activities like improv class make you an active participant in the center of the experience rather than a passive observer. We learn far more about ourselves when we choose to participate than when we merely consume.

PART
TWO

9. THE THREE GAPS: EFFORT, SKILL AND QUALITY

The great surprise for people with good ideas is the gap between how an idea feels in their mind and how it feels when they put the idea to work. When a good idea comes together it feels fantastic. Good ideas often come with a wave of euphoria, a literal dopamine high, and we're joyously overwhelmed by it. It's natural in that instant to overlook the dozens of questions that must be answered to bring the idea to life. We easily postpone those questioning thoughts, believing that if we can come up with the big idea surely we can conquer all the little problems too. An epiphany is a powerful experience, but the **myth of epiphany** is that it alone is all you need.[13]

When we do sit down to work on the details of an idea, the euphoria fades away. The act of thinking about how to bring the idea into the world is far less fun than the magical feeling of the idea's arrival. It might take an hour or a day, but soon the tasks at hand feel surprisingly ordinary. While the 30-second summary of your science fiction screenplay is still fantastic, it doesn't eliminate the effort required to write three, or more, complete drafts to flesh the idea out into its final form. Even if your idea was for your job, perhaps an inspiring new proposal you have for your boss, the work of drafting the required project plans and obtaining budget approvals just isn't very interesting. This is the **effort gap**. No

---

[13] Scott Berkun, "The Myth of Epiphany," http://scottberkun.com/2015/the-myth-of-epiphany/.

matter how great your idea is, there will be energy you have to spend, often on relatively ordinary work, to deliver it to the world.

The instinctive reaction to the realization that your amazing idea has led to ordinary work is to retreat. We feel we are doing something wrong if delivering on the idea isn't as stimulating as finding the idea itself. Somehow we believe the feeling of euphoria should remain throughout the entire project, and when it doesn't, and we have to choose to put effort in, we assume something is amiss. In the movies they often skip from the discovery of the idea to fame and fortune, but in real life we have to close that distance ourselves.[14] Or perhaps more honestly we simply don't want to work that hard, preferring to return to the thrills of thinking up more ideas ra-

---

[14] Ibid.

ther than doing anything about them. There is nothing wrong with this, as dreaming for dreams' sake can be fun. The problem is when we torture ourselves by denying the fact that we have less ambition than we wish we had.

Many people suffer from creative cowardice and a fear of commitment. They are afraid of closing the effort gap. They want to be creative but without any risks. They know there is a chance they can put in weeks of work and have the project fail. So they prefer the shallow perfection of keeping the idea locked in their minds, taking it out only to stroke their ego and annoy their friends. When someone else produces something with a similar idea, perhaps a movie or an invention, they'll claim false possession, exclaiming, "I thought of that years ago!" But the only way to possess an idea is by closing the effort gap and actually putting something out into the world. Coming up with the idea, it turns out, is often the easy part.

Sometimes the problem is the recognition that while the idea is excellent, and you're willing to put the effort in, the skills you have aren't good enough to deliver on it. The natural assumption is that the capacity to have the idea is the harder part, and if the idea is good it implies you have all the required abilities. Sadly, like many common assumptions of our silly little brains, the reality isn't as kind. For example, while I can imagine performing quadruple backflip dives and singing five-octave melodies, that imagination has no bearing on my body's ability to do those things. This is the **skill gap**, the distance between the skills your idea requires and the ones you have. Often it's only through putting effort into a project that we discover our skill gaps.

When we see work from our heroes, it's easy to forget they once had skill gaps too. We imagine they were born with the abilities we know them for. The problem is our view of other creators is inverted. We know them after they became famous and after they learned their craft. The works we know best are rarely an artist's early works but rather those considered masterpieces. When we see a Georgia O'Keeffe painting in a museum, or a J.R.R. Tolkien novel in the bookstore, we see the creators at their best and likely in their prime. We don't see their many experiments, their uncertain output during the long years they developed the skills they'd become famous for. As Steven Furtick said, "The reason we struggle with insecurity is because we compare our behind-the-scenes with everyone else's highlight reel." We have to go out of our way to find their behind-the-scenes work, and often we forget it even exists.

Ira Glass, host of *This American Life*, explained how these skill gaps work against us[15]:

"*Nobody tells people who are beginners, and I really wish someone had told this to me... all of us who do creative work, we get into it because we have good taste.... there's a gap... for the first couple years that you're making stuff, what you're making isn't so good.... It's not that great.... It's trying to be good, it has ambition to be good, but it's not quite that good.*

But your taste, the thing that got you into the game, is still killer. And your taste is good enough that you can tell that what you're making is kind of a disappointment to you.... A lot of people never get past this phase.... they quit.

And the thing I would say to you with all my heart is that most everybody I know who does interesting creative work, they went

---

[15] Ira Glass on Storytelling, part 3, https://www.youtube.com/watch?v=X2wLPoizeJE

*through a phase of years [of this]....
Everybody goes through that.... And the most
important possible thing you can do is do a
lot of work. Do a huge volume of work... it's
only by actually going through a volume of
work that you are actually going to catch up
and close that gap. And the work you're making will be as good as your ambitions."*

Many talented people never develop
their skills because they hate the feeling
of this distance. They're embarrassed
and tortured by it. They expect to
improve at a pace born only from
wishful thinking, and when they fail to
meet it they despair. They lack the
commitment required to find out,
through practice, exactly how much skill
they might be capable of. Instead they
want an easy and guaranteed path
despite the fact that none of the heroes
they compare themselves against ever
had one. The tough news that Ira Glass
hints at is that it's easier for our
ambitions to grow, as that happens

simply by consuming good works, than it is for our skills to improve, something that requires dedicated effort.

One way to stay motivated in closing skill gaps is to study the history of masters you admire. The early works of Claude Monet and Jackson Pollock are drastically different from the styles they became most famous for. Brad Pitt's first "acting role" was in a chicken costume for a Mexican fast food restaurant.[16] Michael Jordan, the basketball legend, was cut from his junior varsity basketball team. And who knows how many lousy plays young Shakespeare wrote that he burned, or poems Emily Dickinson tore apart and buried in the dust? Honest biographies of nearly every famous musician, writer or entrepreneur will share in painful de-

---

[16] Jonny Black, "Brad Pitt Facts," *Moviefone*, October 17, 2014, https://www.moviefone.com/2014/10/17/brad-pitt-facts/.

tail how they worked to close the skill gaps in their careers.

Once you've developed your skills, how you choose to use them is a matter of style. Style, or quality, gaps are the most subjective of all. Unlike effort and skill gaps, a **quality gap** is a subjective opinion of the quality of what is made. When J.K. Rowling filled five pages of made-up Q words, it wasn't because of a lack of skill. There was a specific quality, a feeling, a tone, an effect she wanted that she struggled to obtain. Each word still didn't feel quite right, so she'd come up with another one (put another way, she solved a quality gap by creating and closing an effort gap).[17] Depending on what idea you have in your mind,

---

[17] The divisions between effort, skill and quality gaps break down eventually. In a way, all gaps are effort gaps, as work must be put in to fill gaps of any kind. But at times it can be useful to ask: do you need to put in more effort? Invest in skill development? Or simply have more patience to get to the quality you desire?

even if you work hard and have the right skills, you will still experience quality gaps as you work on projects.

Some legendary creators struggled with their own opinion of their work, even after their public success. No matter how popular they became, they felt their work was flawed, inferior and immature, never reaching the standards set in their own minds. Woody Allen rarely watches his films once they're finished, and thinks little of *Manhattan* and *Annie Hall*, two of his most famous works. Bruce Springsteen once called the *Born To Run* album "the worst piece of garbage" he'd ever heard, and didn't want to release it.[18] Nabokov hated many of his novels, and had thrown the

[18] Louis P. Masur, "Tramps like Us: The Birth of *Born to Run*," *Slate*, September 22, 2009, http://www.slate.com/articles/arts/music_box/2009/09/tramps_like_us.2.html.

manuscript for *Lolita* into a fire.[19] Franz Kafka and Emily Dickinson both gave instructions to have all their work destroyed when they died. Artists are often victims in a way of their own perceived quality gaps. They struggle to match the ideas in their minds to what they can manifest in the world.

Some very successful creators never close the quality gap, at least not on every project, and you likely won't either. This is fine, perhaps even good. If you want to keep growing it demands that when you finish a project you'll see it differently than when you started. And in the very things you find lacking or wish you had done differently you find the motivation for the next project,

---

[19] George Lowery, "Vladimir and Vera Nabokov had 'mystifying' relationship, Schiff Says," *Cornell Chronicle*, June 23, 2006, http://www.news.cornell.edu/stories/2006/06/vladimir-and-vera-nabokov-had-mystifying-relationship-schiff-says.

and the one after that. To be perfectly satisfied with something you made likely means you didn't learn anything along the way, and I'd rather be a little disappointed with projects now and then than experience the alternative of never learning anything at all.

These three gaps, effort, skill and quality, will be constant companions. Have patience in how you deal with them. Consider yourself part of a challenging trade where it takes time to develop your craft and that development never ends. If you truly believe in your ideas and potential, you should be willing to stay the course and commit to the long, and only realistic, path to fulfilling your ambitions.

If you can, take pleasure in making things for the sake of making them: what a gift to have the time to make at all! If you were born 200 years ago, or to different parents in a different country, you wouldn't have the time to feel bad about your work, because you wouldn't have the wealth and time required to try. If you feel love for your craft, honor it by showing up, even when it's hard. Especially when it's hard. Working when it's hardest often teaches rare lessons that will earn you easy rides now and then. Take pleasure in small progressions when you see them, and know those hard-won gains are the only way anyone in history has ever achieved anything noteworthy—for themselves or for the world.

10. THE DISCIPLINE

Pete Maravich was one of the most inventive basketball players of all time. He is in the Basketball Hall of Fame because of how creative he was in finding ways to score, pass and dribble. If you watch highlight videos of him playing, it seems as if he was born to do what he did, making the ball move as if it were on a string that only he could see. He seemed to be a different kind of creature, able to do things on the court that no other player could.

The terms *natural* or *prodigy* are often used to describe someone who has, what must be, extraordinary talent. But when you study the history of people who are granted these labels, the surprise is you almost always find a very disciplined, or at least obsessive, person. As a teenager Maravich kept a basketball with him all the time, dribbling in the hallways at school, on his way home and even in movie theaters (surely a creative way to ensure no one sits near you).[20] As the legend goes, he even slept with a basketball in his bed. Jimi Hendrix, although he had no formal lessons, played his guitar as often as he could, even while he served in the Army. Stories of their dedication aren't as popular as ones about their "magical talent," yet there's no story of a person who had one without the other.

Too often we are distracted away from what we say is important by things that are more pleasurable or convenient. This means a central skill any creative person needs is a mastery of time, which means a mastery of habits. There will always be easier things in our lives than creative work. There will always be demands on our time that are more logical and lucrative than chasing an

---

[20] Mark Kriegel, *Pistol: The Life of Pete Maravich* (New York: Free Press, 2007), pg. 66.

idea. If you are truly passionate about something you must be willing to make sacrifices to make it possible. What good is that passion if you can't use it to help you do the work? Merely saying you are passionate, or feeling passionate, is not enough.

The simplest habit is to work on your project every day. If you don't have a project, go to your private journal or drawing notebook daily until you do. It can be for ten minutes or an hour, but you must touch the work at least once a day. It can be in the morning, or late at night, or during your lunch break at work. At first when and where won't matter. All that counts is that you commit to the discipline of honoring your ideas. People have written entire novels in prison (*Don Quixote* by Cervantes), or by getting up early before going to work (*The Bluest Eye* by Toni Morrison). They simply wanted to do it enough to be dedicated to the task, sacrificing the limited free time they had. If there is no sacrifice there is no discipline, and if there is no discipline there is no progress. It can be, as artist Patti Smith says, "a joyful sacrifice," where you think more about what you are doing than what you are giving up, but either way you must put in the time.[21]

Many people say, "This idea is very important to me, but I don't have time." This is a lie because importance is relative. You can only call a pursuit, such as writing poems or making music, important if you identify what is less important and what you are willing to give up. We all have the same time limit of 24 hours every day, which means the difference between a productive creative person and an unsatisfied dreamer is in how they choose to use it. Most of us

---

[21] "Patti Smith Never Wanted To Be Famous," *Here's The Thing* podcast, December 27, 2016, http://www.wnyc.org/story/patti-smith-never-wanted-to-be-famous.

forget how much of our time goes to entertainment, things we do purely for pleasure. We have plenty of time—it's just we have to protect it for the things we claim are most important.

The simplest habit of discipline is to make a little chart. It can be on paper or a computer, as long as it's something you are forced to look at every day (mine is on a whiteboard in my office, in direct view of my desk). Make a box for each day of the week. Every day that you work on your project, or simply open your journal, you mark off the box for that day. Soon you'll have two days in a row. Then five. The momentum and pride you feel will help compel you to keep the streak going. And when you miss a day, you'll be angry with yourself, and can use that anger to make sure you show up the next day to start another streak. Many professionals, including Jerry Seinfeld, use a simple technique like this to keep their focus on what matters most.[22]

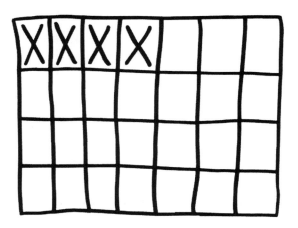

If you discover you have discipline, and can show up every day, but have nothing to say, don't worry. There are many excellent books of games and simple methods for coming up with

---

[22] Gina Trapani, "Jerry Seinfeld's Productivity Secret," *Lifehacker*, July 24, 2007, http://lifehacker.com/281626/jerry-seinfelds-productivity-secret.

ideas. *Cracking Creativity* by Michael Michalko is one of my favorites, but there are many others. The musician and artist Brian Eno created a deck of creativity cards, called *Oblique Strategies*, that challenges you to create. But as I mentioned in Part 1, it turns out you don't need many methods if you have discipline. What's more important is to commit to show up, every day, and give your instincts a chance to surface. If you have discipline, you will have good habits, and nothing will stand in your way.

In the book *Daily Rituals: How Artists Work*, Mason Currey explains that "A solid routine fosters a well-worn groove for one's mental energies and helps stave off the tyranny of moods." The investment in good habits is one of the best we can make. It rewards us with protection against the forces, both within and outside us, that tempt us away from our deepest ambitions.

11. WHY YOU GET IDEAS (IN THE SHOWER)

If you forced me to give you a step-by-step method for creativity, I'd point you to the one defined by psychologist Mihaly Csikszentmihalyi.[23] You probably won't like it, but that's what happens when you force people to give you things. He defines it in five steps:

1. **Preparation**: Study a subject, identify ideas, become immersed in the topic or subject that aroused your curiosity.
2. **Incubation**: Ideas churn around below the threshold of consciousness.
3. **Insight**: Your subconscious mind makes connections.

---

[23] Mihaly Csikszentmihalyi, *Creativity: Flow and the Psychology of Discovery and Invention* (New York: Harper Perennial, 2013).

4. **Evaluation**: Decide which, if any, of the insights are worth pursuing.
5. **Elaboration**: Develop the ideas into the final work.

You could take everything I've told you in this book so far and put it into one of his five categories. The category I find most entertaining is his last one, Elaboration. It's a nice five-syllable word that sounds impressive, and like the diagrams I warned you about earlier, five-syllable words often skip over the hard parts. To develop an idea into "the final work" could take months, years or not ever be possible even with a billion dollars and a dream team of Einstein, da Vinci and Margaret Atwood. Yet it only earns a single cute little sentence in the list above.

I've referenced this step-by-step method because of a promise I made early in this book. After making fun of the question "Where do ideas come from?" I explained that their source is our minds, and in particular our subconscious. Steps 2 and 3, Incubation and Insight, are critical in explaining how this works, as well as what we should do to work with our brains instead of against them.

You will discover that after an hour of coming up with ideas, combining them and perhaps sketching some out, you simply get tired. You've used up whatever capacity you have to explore. What most people don't know is that this is just the first wave. You will need your subconscious to provide the second wave (and future ones). To help it get started, the best thing you can do is to leave the project alone and do something else. I know this sounds ridiculous. "So we're supposed to go walk the dog or wash dishes while we wait for our subconscious minds to get busy?" Yes, you are. This is twice as maddening a prospect to accept if you are on a deadline, but your subconscious cares little about rational problems like deadlines or not getting fired.

You'll find many creative people dedicate time every day for being idle. They go for walks, they stare out windows or they sit in the café, sip coffee and observe. Maybe they chat with friends over beers or a game of cards. To any rational person this seems lazy, as they are not "working" in the strictest sense. But as Csikszentmihalyi researched, these habits are not frivolous. When our conscious minds have less to do, there's more room for our subconscious mind to work at both processing the thoughts we've thought about recently, and finding new ideas to report back to us. This *incubation*, time spent doing something where our minds can wander, accelerates creativity. It's counterintuitive, but why would we expect creativity to be logical and rational?

People are often mystified by the magical powers taking a shower provides in delivering solutions to problems they've been stuck on for days. The creative potency of taking a shower has little to do with the shower itself. It's simply that in modern life we have few places where we are not bombarded by incoming information. During most waking hours we multitask, putting one layer of activity for our brains on top of another. We "watch" television while we browse social media on our phones. There's little time for our minds to review what we've already experienced, much less to process it, shape it and make connections. The shower is one of the few places left that we all must go where there are no advertisements, no news, no screens and no input for our minds. We relax, we sink back into the comfort of our bodies, and our brains slowly recover from everything we've asked them to do all day long.

If you want to think well, you need to make your behavior line up closer to how our brains actually function. There are many different kinds of passive activities other than bathing that have similar effects. Going for a jog, practicing yoga and hiking in the woods all work just as well, at least for some people. There is good evidence that for many of us it's physical activity, kinesthesis or moving our bodies, that helps our minds find a more productive state, both for our conscious and subconscious thinking. This makes sense, evolutionarily speaking: one hundred thousand years ago, when did we need to have our sharpest wits? It was probably when we were being chased by hungry, sharp-clawed beasts (a motivating experience that parallels the psychology of being trapped in a closet). Our brains are designed to think while in motion, so use what once was a survival trait to your advantage. Niels Bohr and Einstein used to go for long walks as they discussed physics problems. They understood the value of moving the body to help move the thoughts in their minds.

Repetitive tasks that don't require much thinking, like peeling potatoes, knitting a sweater or mowing the lawn, might work too. Since everyone's psychology is different, it will be a different kind of passive task that works best for you. The good news is you now have a reason to put more pleasurable and relaxing activities into your life, something you should probably do more of anyway.

12. THE TIGHTROPE OF CREATIVE CONFIDENCE

To get off the couch and do something interesting requires confidence. The more interesting the goal, the more confidence you need. But if you have too much confidence, you'll be blind to the lessons you need to learn to make something as good as what you imagined in your mind. Too much confidence means you won't ask for feedback, do sufficient research or look for collaborators even when you need one. But on the other hand, if you have too little confidence, you either won't get off the couch or you'll give up too easily.

The balance you need to find is to be confident but not *too* confident. To possess the self-control to act in a bold or doubtful way whenever you wish, mastering the tightrope of your own mind. During the creative dances you will be doing, you may need to force yourself to keep going (past inhibition), or force yourself to stop (to aid your subconscious mind). How do you know for sure which is the right choice? You don't! Once again, welcome to the fun of being someone who makes new things.

It's useful to have in your possession the lens of the devil's advocate, questioning and doubting the thing you just made. Does this solve the problem? What is missing? How else could I do this? By asking questions about your work you'll discover new paths you'd have never seen if you just assumed it was perfect. Feedback from other people can help raise those questions if you're confident enough to ask them for their honest opinions.

But you also need the angel's advocate, which can see the best in something ("What is this good for?"). If you spend too much time challenging what you currently have, you'll never get to the next revision. You need to have strong faith in the next draft, that you will be a little smarter and wiser by the time this draft is finished and your only responsibility is to get there. In a way, the draft you write now is a gift to the future version of you.

People who make things walk these tightropes often. They develop a meta-confidence, a trust that while they may go too far one way or the other, they'll recognize it eventually and correct themselves. You will never be perfect walking this tightrope. You will sometimes fall from having too much confidence and from having not enough. You will face times when you find it hard to see your work in more than one way. This is the life of a creative mind. The way forward is not to hate the rope, but to be grateful for how it will always challenge you to pay attention, learn and grow. You'll discover that no matter how many things you've made, the next project will challenge you in new ways.

If you keep returning to the tightrope, you will continue to learn more about the world and yourself for the rest of your life.

13. FEEDBACK VS. ENCOURAGEMENT

It's natural for a project you've worked on to be personally important to you. Unlike most ordinary work, like shoveling dirt or stacking boxes, creating something born from our minds makes us feel our identity is imbued into the thing we've made. As a result, many people are sensitive about their creative projects. We respond to critiques, even constructive ones, as if we have been personally attacked. Somehow in the hard work of putting ourselves into the project, we have trouble pulling ourselves back out. This is a tragedy of self-limitation. It reduces the number of new insights we are able to see, or that people will be willing to share with us.

In a way, we set a trap for ourselves every time we show our work to other people. We may ask, "What do you think of this leak-proof faucet I designed?" when in our hearts we are asking a rhetorical question like, "Isn't this brilliant and aren't I amazing to choose to spend my time making something like this?" The first question truly asks for an opinion. The second question, the one in our hearts, fishes for support for who we are as a person. And in the huge psychological difference between these two kinds of questions, everyone is likely to suffer.

When we set this trap and someone gives us an honest, but less than positive, answer to the first question we get upset. We take it as a judgment of who we are rather than simply a critique of this one particular project we made. And when we get visibly upset because our feelings have been hurt, the other person is justifiably confused. They are trying to help, but as they sense our hurt they feel surprised and confused and are unlikely to ever give us honest feedback again. Next time they'll simply say, "It looks great" regardless of their actual opinion.

You must learn to separate feedback, which is about the work you've made, from encouragement, which is about you as a person. Always be clear in your mind what you are asking for, and make sure it's clear to the person you're asking.

There are five ways to improve the quality of feedback you get:

- **Who you ask**. Friends are easy people to ask, but do they know much about the kind of work you do? Will they be honest? Can they be thoughtful? A person with these traits will yield better feedback than simply someone you get along with well. It takes time to find people who have the perspective you need and the trust in you to tell you the truth. You need to cultivate relationships that have all of these traits. Ask for input on something small, push them to be truthful and then genuinely reward them. Repeat this, and over time you'll earn one of the greatest assets a creative person can have.

- **How you ask**. Ask a vague question and you'll get a vague answer. Make sure they understand the particular notion of good you are aiming for. Tell them the goal you were trying to achieve to help them frame their feedback. Ask focused questions like, "How can I make this better?" or "Does this solve these three objectives or have these two qualities?" This gives the other person a menu of thoughts to work from instead of starting from scratch in crafting their opinion.

- **When you ask**. If you want thoughtful feedback, give people time to provide it. If you catch someone in the office hallway and shove a faucet in their face, you're assuming they want to be interrupted from everything else they planned to do that day. You'll get more thoughtful feedback if the timing of when you ask is thoughtful and on their terms, not yours.

- **Where you ask**. We are social creatures and behave differently depending on where we are. You will get different feedback from someone if they are rushing to get to work, or are relaxing over a beer at happy hour.

- **How you respond**. Everyone assumes they handle feedback well, but few do. We debate, we argue and we brood. We instinctively find it hard to believe other people don't see what we see, and assume we can wrestle them into seeing it. If you truly want to learn anything, you must shut up and listen. Don't convince, but do try to learn. Ask better questions to probe their opinion rather than try to change it. For example, if you told me you hated this chapter, I could ask, "Do you think it should be shorter, revised to be more insightful, or killed completely?"

I've found that tough feedback is easier to hear if I keep in mind that I'm working not only on the current project but on improving my intuition for all future projects too. This reminds me I can't be too precious about what I've made *this* time if I expect to make more in the future (preciousness is a subject we will explore soon). The only way I can grow is to put something out in front of others and learn from what they experience.

Unlike feedback, which is about acquiring new insights, encouragement is for you as a person. Your morale is important, and encouragement is one source of fuel for it. It's powerful to know that support can be obtained without anyone liking your work at all. Vincent van Gogh's only real encouragement for the decade he worked as an artist was his brother, who rarely critiqued his work but provided money, advice and a belief that what he was doing was worthwhile. If you want encouragement, ask for it. Tell a friend that you're not motivated, or stuck, or sad, or whatever emotional experience you're having that's not helping you work. This frames the conversation differently and puts the focus on how you feel rather than on what you are working on.

You will discover some people are excellent at giving feedback and others are great at providing encouragement. Of course, many people are terrible at both. Lastly, there are a handful of magic ninja unicorns that can do both well and perhaps even know what you need at a particular moment better than you do (and often ask, before they say anything else, "Do you really want a critique or do you want encouragement?"). It's up to you as a creator to cultivate relationships with people to meet the needs you have. When you find people who are good at these roles, cherish them. They are hard to find.

14. HOW TO BE A GENIUS

Among the many abused words around creative work is the word *genius*. Generally geniuses don't exist in the present. Think of all the people you've ever met: would you call any of them a genius, in the Mozart, Einstein or Shakespeare sense of the word? Even the commonly called genius grants from the MacArthur Foundation shy away from actually calling their recipients geniuses. Most people throw the g-word around where it's safe: in reference to dead people. Since there's no one alive who witnessed young Mozart pee in his pants or saw young Einstein eating crayons in kindergarten, we can call them geniuses in safety, as their humanity has been stripped away from our conception of them.

Even if you believe geniuses exist, there's little consensus as to what it means to be a genius. Some experts say genius is the capacity for greatness, while others believe it's that you've accomplished great things. Frankly, I don't think you should care. You can't accomplish much as a maker of things if your time is spent arguing about the meaning of words like *genius* (or *creativity* itself). What we really want is a better understanding of how to appreciate, and possibly become, interesting people. To do this requires digging into their daily lives and working habits, as it's their work we are most interested in.

For years I've read histories of famous creative legends in many fields to improve my understanding of how great works are made. And I can offer you this manic, entertaining stroll through the contradictory and often disturbing truths I've discovered.

Have a Great or Horrible Family

Picasso, Mozart, Beethoven and Einstein are four popular geniuses with parents who took an interest in their creative lives. Mozart and Beethoven had fathers who were professional musicians, and at young ages they were taught how to read music and play various instruments. Can you guess what Picasso's dad did? Yes, he was a painter, and spent many hours with young Pablo showing him the ropes. One popular legend around Einstein is his young obsession with a compass from his dad, but more significant for his development was family friend Max Talmud, who taught Albert science, philosophy and other intellectual pursuits throughout his boyhood. The late singer Prince had dual musical influences, as his father played piano and his mother was a jazz singer. And of course there's van Gogh and his brother Theo, the only healthy relationship he ever had.

But lousy families can produce geniuses too. Beethoven's dad was abusive and cruel, torturing him during childhood practice sessions. Yet unlike what happens to most child prodigies— who burn out at age 15 and develop a complete hatred for their gifts and micromanaging, self-centered parents— somehow Beethoven's passion for music survived. Leonardo da Vinci was a "bastard", a child not of any of his father's eventual four wives, and the little we know doesn't paint a picture (ha ha) of a healthy child-parent dynamic. Isaac Newton was also born to a single-parent home, his father dying several weeks before Isaac entered the world. When his mother remarried, Isaac didn't like it, and perhaps thus found a seed of unrest to fuel his pursuit of an independent life.

I'm fond of the ideas of independence, free will and the belief anyone can do anything, but when it comes to being a genius it's hard to ignore the role of family, country and era—all things out of an individual's control. If Mozart's dad had been a rat catcher or Beethoven's a chimney sweeper, what would have happened? Had Emily Dickinson's mother not been seriously ill for decades, forcing Emily to live mostly in seclusion, would we know her name? Put young Steve Jobs or Elon Musk in the London slums during the Great Plague of 1665, and the course of their lives would be different indeed.

Whether positive or negative, opportunities during children's development create potential, but their work has to surface at a time when their particular talents are valued in the world (as demonstrated by the number of posthumously appreciated geniuses, including Tesla, Kafka, van Gogh and Dickinson).

Be Obsessed with Work

Show me a genius and I'll show you a workaholic. Van Gogh produced 2,000 works of art between 1880 and 1890 (1,100 paintings and 900 sketches). That's four works of art a week for a decade, and he didn't start making art until his mid-twenties. Da Vinci's famous journals represent decades of notetaking, doodling and observations, and it's a good guess that work was the center of his life: no spouses or children are mentioned in any of our records of him (though he likely had lovers in his studio). Picasso made over 12,000 works of art in his lifetime ("Give me a museum and I'll fill it," he said, and he was right), including sculptures, paintings and other mediums. Shakespeare wrote more than 30 plays, not to mention dozens of sonnets, poems and of course, grocery lists. Every art or music prodigy practiced to produce the work they are famous for. While they had great flourishes of ability, their talents were grounded in effort. Van Gogh was fond of quoting the painter James Whistler, who once said, "it took me two hours to do, but forty years to learn how to do it in two hours." These are people who practiced their crafts daily and sacrificed many other ordinary pleasures in life to make their work possible.

And of course very few of these works are considered masterpieces, by their creators or anyone else. Sure, today, any coffee-stained sketch by Picasso or van Gogh garners millions, but that has more to do with the signature that's on the painting than the quality of the painting itself. No matter the field, the productive have more failures to show than successes by ratios of ten or more to one.

Hemingway is noted for his belief that writing is rewriting, and that dozens or hundreds of attempts are required to write anything well. (He once said, "The first draft of anything is shit."[24]) Most painters, from Dali to Turner, made sketches and studies to experiment and explore before committing themselves to the final versions of the amazing works we see in museums. Even Michelangelo spent long hours sketching and experimenting with different approaches to his sculptures, but wanting to preserve the romantic notion of his genius, he burned nearly all of the papers these test works were written on.

Whatever their talents or genetic gifts, most everyone who earned the label genius was dedicated to their work: the list of lazy geniuses is short. The debate over talent versus work ethic is moot in history: without the work, we'd never have heard of any of these people. By the law of averages there have been

---

[24] Many quotes from famous people are misattributed or fake. This one seems real. http://quoteinvestigator.com/2015/09/20/draft/

hundreds of people who had more talent and opportunity than these legends had but who simply didn't have the same commitment to closing their effort gaps, and spent more of their lifetime doing other things.

Have Emotional or Other Serious Problems

A high percentage of geniuses weren't particularly happy, well-adjusted people. Success and happiness have a surprisingly low correlation it seems, despite how American culture has blended them together. It'd be unfair to say being unhappy is a requirement, but there's sure evidence for a correlation. For all their brilliance, it doesn't seem like most of these people led stable lives. Picasso, van Gogh, Edison, Einstein and Nietzsche (not to mention almost every major modern philosopher) had difficult, if not disastrous, personal lives. Every one of them either never married or married many times, had children they abandoned or became estranged from, and had episodes of great depression and turmoil. Isaac Newton and Tesla spent many of their days in isolation and had enough eccentricities and personality disorders to earn a cabinet full of pharmaceuticals today. Sylvia Plath, Kurt Cobain and dozens of other genius-level creators committed suicide, a reflection of the torment they felt toward existence itself.

Michelangelo and da Vinci were troublesome employees, abandoning commissions from popes and bishops, fleeing cities because of threats of war and debt collectors. Franz Kafka and Marcel Proust were both notable hypochondriacs, each spending years of their lives in bed or in hospitals for medical conditions, some of which were psychological in nature or origin. Voltaire, Thoreau and Socrates all lived in various kinds of exile or poverty, and used their responses to these conditions in the works they are famous for. Positive emotions and experiences can work as fuel, too; there just don't seem to be as many genius stories that center on happy, well-adjusted lives. John Coltrane, C.S. Lewis and Einstein had deeply held, and mostly positive, spiritual beliefs that fueled their work. Stephen King seems like a happy person at his core, despite all the horror that passes through his mind.

Emotions of any kind, positive or negative, provide fuel for work (and for closing effort gaps). Many geniuses were simply better at converting their emotions into work than their peers. The need to express feelings, escape suffering or prove the possibility of an imagined world was stronger in these people than the challenges of the work itself, enabling them to spend more of their waking hours searching for expression or solving problems than most people choose to. Creativity and self-expression are hard work for anyone, but perhaps a lesson we can learn from the prolific is to widen our sources of fuel and raise our tolerance for hard work.

Don't Strive for Fame in Your Lifetime

This is the killer for the ego, but most geniuses had a fraction of the fame in their lifetimes compared to what they received after their deaths. Kafka, Darwin, Melville, Edgar Allan Poe and van Gogh all died young, poor and with moderate (and in Kafka, Melville and van Gogh's cases, near zero) fame for their talents. It's possible that desiring legend status in your lifetime will spoil whatever magic you have, as you end up aiming for shallow targets. This theory explains why many people have a single amazing work but never return to the same artistic, intellectual or creative brilliance in their later efforts. The attention of their fields, or the world at large, may create more pressure than they can manage. The list of suicides and young deaths among brilliant creators is painfully long, including Jim Morrison, Elvis Presley, Kurt Cobain, van Gogh, Hemingway, Hunter S. Thompson, Sylvia Plath, Virginia Woolf, Alan Turing, John Coltrane, John Belushi, Chet Baker, Jackson Pollock—the list goes on.

Perhaps it's best not to care what the world thinks, or what labels it gives you, and focus on independence as the true seed for making great things worthy of, someday, earning you the moniker of genius. To focus on the making, the thinking, the creating seems the best way, leaving it to the world to decide, long after you're gone, what value your work had. As long as you're free enough to keep making and creating in ways that satisfy your personal ambitions, or perhaps the taste of a handful of fans, you're doing much better than most people ever have.

15. DON'T BE PRECIOUS (WITH YOUR IDEAS)

Being precious means you're behaving as if the draft, the sketch, the idea you're working on is the most important thing in the history of the universe. It means you've lost perspective and can't see the work objectively anymore. When you treat a work in progress too preciously, you trade your talents for fears. You become conservative, suppressing the courage required to make the tough choices needed to resolve the work's problems and let you finish. If you fear that your next decision will ruin the work, you are being precious.

When I see a young writer struggling to finish a book or a painter wrestling with an incomplete painting, I say, "Don't be precious," something the artist Teresa Brazen once told me. It means that if you truly love your craft, there is an infinite number of projects in your future. There will be other chapters. There will be other canvases and other songs. Perfection is a prison and a self-made one. Whatever you're making, it doesn't have to be perfect. Perfection is an illusion.

Obsessing about every choice is a surefire way to prevent great work from happening. Try a bold choice instead. Put the beginning at the end or the top at the bottom. Blow up your work into jagged pieces and put them back together. You might just find this opens doors you didn't even know existed. If you're too precious, you miss the hundreds of big choices that might reveal the path to completion, or convince you the project is a puzzle that needs to be abandoned for a time. But if you spin your wheels faster and faster on smaller and smaller details, you'll never move anywhere. You're working against the natural dance of possibilities. Perhaps you'll never call anything finished, denying yourself the essential experience of looking back from a distance and learning from what you've already made.

Some Buddhist monks make mandalas, intricate paintings made from colored grains of sand placed individually on a wide canvas. When completed, the mandalas are destroyed. These monks create and then wipe away these wondrous works to remind themselves not to be too precious—not only about their works of art but about life itself. This isn't an excuse not to work hard. Mandalas take great skill and patience to create. Instead, it's a recognition that while your work might mean everything to you in the moment, in the grand scheme of your career, your life and the universe itself, it's just another thing that will someday fade away.

Of course, it is important to strive for greatness. You should care deeply about ideas that matter to you. There's a long history of masters, from Michelangelo to Twyla Tharp to Stanley Kubrick, who obsessed about the smallest details of their works and demanded the best from everyone who worked with them. In some ways, they were very precious and demanding. But they didn't let those ambitions stop them from finishing their works: if they had stayed stuck forever on a single project in their obsession for detail, we wouldn't know their names. Productive masters know how to be both intimate with and distant from their own work. We all need to learn the same flexibility. It's healthy for you, and for progress in your craft, not to obsess too much over what you make.

All good makers leave a legacy of abandoned drafts, unfinished works, mediocre projects and failed ideas, work that enabled them to learn what they needed to finish the projects they are famous for. If your high standards or self-loathing are preventing your progress, don't be precious about it. It takes hundreds of experiences with the cycle of starting, working and finishing creative works before you have the talent to complete things that match the grandeur of the ideas in your mind.

Say "don't be precious" to yourself when you're stuck. Let your obsession go, or dismantle it into fun-sized pieces and let the chips fall where they may. Move on, learn and repeat. You're a creator, which means you can make the ordinary into the interesting whenever you want. There are multitudes of projects ahead in your life, but you can only get to them if you move past the one you are making far too precious now.

PART
THREE

16. CREATIVITY IS NOT AN ACCIDENT

A common pattern of the **myth of epiphany**, the false belief that flashes of insight matter more than everything else, is creativity by accident. The very idea of the Muses, mystical forces that choose to grant ideas to us from above, externalizes creativity, and accidents have a similar appeal. Since we're all often victims of accidents, we're attracted to stories that redeem accidents by turning them into break-throughs. Newton watching an apple fall, an ordinary event anyone could observe, is perhaps the greatest example of this kind of misleading storytelling. It took him years of work to describe the mathematics of gravity regardless of the apple's disputed epiphanistic potency.

Many major magazines and movies tell stories that glorify "creativity by accident." For example, here's a quote from a recent article, "How To Cultivate the Art of Serendipity," in *The New York Times*[25]:

"*In 2008, an inventor named Steve Hollinger lobbed a digital camera across his studio toward a pile of pillows. "I wasn't trying to make an invention," he said. "I was just playing." As his camera flew, it recorded what most of us would call a bad photo. But when Mr. Hollinger peered at that blurry image, he saw new possibilities. Soon, he was building a throwable video camera in the shape of a baseball, equipped with gyroscopes and sensors.*"

A quick read of Hollinger's own page about the invention (called a Serveball) reveals important facts that distinguish him from most of us:

---

[25] Pagan Kennedy, "How To Cultivate the Art of Serendipity," *The New York Times*, January 2, 2016, http://www.nytimes.com/2016/01/03/opinion/how-to-cultivate-the-art-of-serendipity.html.

- He was a professional inventor and artist, successful enough to be profiled by Susan Orlean in *The New Yorker* in 2008.
- He had a workshop for inventing things, including a rig for camera experiments.
- He worked over the course of a year on this project, a period of time Kennedy refers to as "soon."

Play is a fantastic use of time and can be very helpful for developing skills for invention and creation. But it's important to note that Hollinger's idea of play is likely different from ours. It's serious play. As Susan Orlean described in *The New Yorker* in 2008,[26] this is no ordinary person:

---

[26] Susan Orlean, "Thinking in the Rain," *The New Yorker*, February 11, 2008, http://www.newyorker.com/magazine/2008/02/11/thinking-in-the-rain.

"He had spent the previous month mostly locked in his apartment, furiously teaching himself the principles of aerodynamics, the physics of hydrology, and the basics of how to operate a Singer sewing machine, and he was at last testing what he had been working on—a reimagined, reinvented umbrella, with gutters and airfoils and the elegant drift of a bird's wing.

There is nothing accidental or serendipitous about locking yourself into an apartment to learn new skills. He was obsessed about this project, like many creators often are about their work. Kennedy continues:

A surprising number of the conveniences of modern life were invented when someone stumbled upon a discovery or capitalized on an accident: the microwave oven, safety glass, smoke detectors, artificial sweeteners, X-ray imaging."

The problem here is the phrase "were invented when." While there was a moment of insight triggered by the accident, it's misleading to suggest that this moment is when the idea came to fruition. In most cases these were experienced scientists, working in experimental laboratories, who had a context for their insight that allowed them to develop it, over months or years, into a true invention. Scratching the surface of each of these stories reveals a much larger investment of effort from the inventors:

- **Microwave oven**. In 1945, Percy Spencer, an engineer at Raytheon, discovered a candy bar had melted in his pocket near radar equipment. He chose to do a series of experiments to isolate why this happened, and discovered microwaves. It would take about another 20 years before the technology developed sufficiently to reach consumers.
- **Safety glass**. In 1903 scientist Edouard Benedictus, while in his lab,

dropped a flask by accident, and to his surprise it did not break. He discovered the flask held residual cellulose nitrate, creating a protective coating. It would be more than a decade before it was used commercially in gas masks.

- **Artificial sweeteners**. Constantin Fahlberg, a German scientist, discovered saccharin, the first artificial sweetener, in 1879. After working in his lab he forgot to wash his hands, and at dinner discovered an exceptionally sweet taste. He returned to his lab, tasting his various experiments until he rediscovered the right one (risking his life in an attempt to understand his accident).

- **Smoke detector**. Walter Jaeger was trying to build a sensor to detect poison gas. It didn't work, and as the story goes, he lit a cigarette and the sensor went off. It could detect smoke particles but not gas. It took the work of other inventors to build on his discovery and make commercial smoke detectors.

• **X-rays**. Wilhelm Röntgen was already working on the effects of cathode rays in 1895 before he actually discovered X-rays. On November 8, 1895, during an experiment, he noticed crystals glowing unexpectedly, and upon further investigation he isolated a new type of light ray.

And even if we grant these stories did involve an accidental discovery, how many accidents by similarly talented and motivated people led to dead ends? Far more. We are victims of survivorship bias in our popularizing of breakthrough stories, giving attention only to successful accidental outcomes while ignoring the majority of accidents and mistakes that led absolutely nowhere.

The myth of epiphany will always be popular, which means for any inspiring story of a breakthrough, we must ask:

- How much work did the creator do before the accident/breakthrough happened?
- How much work did they do after the accident/breakthrough to understand it?
- What did they sacrifice (time / money / reputation) to convince others of the value of the discovery?
- How many months or years of work were required to develop the idea into its final useful form?

In answering these four questions about any creativity story in the news, however accidental or deliberate, we discover useful habits to emulate.

The one constant is that work is the essential element in all finished creative projects and inventions. No matter how brilliant the idea or miraculous its discovery, work is required to develop it to the point of completion, much less consumption by the rest of the world. The unknown cannot be predictable, and if creativity is an act of discovery, then uncertainty must come with the territory.

Curiosity is a simpler concept than serendipity and far more useful. Curious people are more likely to expend the effort to find the answer to a question on their mind. Successful creative pursuits require an active curiosity and a desire to do experiments and make mistakes— the ability to realize that each mistake can offer a kind of insight, however small, just waiting to be revealed.

17. WHAT IF THE WORLD HATES YOUR IDEAS

A good rule for creative work is to expect to be rejected. You will be. It will happen no matter how successful you are. In fact, there's a good argument that the more popularity you find the more dislike for your work that will come along with it. Take, for example, *The Great Gatsby*, one of the most respected works of American literature in the 20th century. It sells nearly 500,000 copies a year, a staggering number for a work created almost 100 years ago. But if you look on Amazon.com, you will find it has more than 200 one-star reviews. How can so many people hate something so widely accepted as being good? The
answer, as you should know, is a question: What is good? We will never have a single universal answer.

Don't fear having your work hated as much as having your work ignored (and you shouldn't be afraid of that either, but more on that shortly). Making something good, in the way you define it, guarantees there will be another person out there who has the opposite definition. If Sally loves the adrenalized violence of Quentin Tarantino's film *Kill Bill*, odds are she probably hates the subtleties of a cultural drama like *Downton Abbey* (which raises the creative question: what would happen if you combined them into a historic drama about an aristocratic family that lives in an MMA dojo and they resolve their conflicts with martial arts?) Of course some people have fantastic taste for what is good and know how to see it in many different forms and styles, but for most people, their preferences lean one way or another, and for every work they love there's a corresponding one in the world they'd hate.

If you read about even the most successful people in any creative field, the stories of rejections are legendary. Writers and musicians laugh about how many rejections they've experienced in their lives. The founders of Google tried to sell their search engine to Yahoo! and Excite, leading companies in the late 1990s, but were turned down. The original *Star Wars* screenplay was rejected by almost every major studio. *Zen and the Art of Motorcycle Maintenance* was turned down over 100 times.

Stephen King, J.K. Rowling and John Grisham all have bestselling works that were initially rejected. Viggo Mortensen, who played Aragorn in *The Lord of The Rings* trilogy, is often asked why he isn't in certain new movies, and he answers that it's not often his choice![27] Even the most famous actors

---

[27] "Viggo Mortensen, From Warrior King to Captain Fantastic," *Here's The Thing* podcast, July 19, 2016, http://www.wnyc.org/story/htt-viggo-mortensen/.

typically audition for roles, competing against other famous and not-so-famous actors for those parts. If you continue to do creative work, you will continue to find people who don't like what you do enough to support you in the way you wish.

In some ways, how you handle rejection is self-selection for creative work: if you can't handle a few rejections from publishers, venture capitalists or coworkers, how will you handle the bad reviews of your finished project? Every rejection is an opportunity to ask a new question: is there another way I could do this? Or, do I even need someone else's support at all? Maybe I can make this thing on my own and publish it myself? In this age nearly all kinds of creation require very little capital to put out into the world. Nothing is stopping you except making a simple choice: to sacrifice money and time to support your idea (which is what you are asking of a publisher, a music label or bank). Maybe the approval you are seeking from others is really something you need to provide yourself.

18. WHAT IF THE WORLD IGNORES YOUR WORK?

It will take many hours of dedicated effort to create something. Therefore, you should create something you, the maker, finds interesting. Why not please yourself? If you want to make something that pleases other people, that's fine too, but realize the desire to do that is still your choice.

"Will anyone care about my work?" people often ask. Yes—you. It starts with you. Many people with an idea want an authority to tell them their idea is worthy. Why is approval necessary? You are the one who is going to do all of the heavy lifting. You can always choose to start your own company, to self-publish or self-produce whatever creation you have in mind. No matter what support you seek, or don't, it will still be you that must put in the time.

If you think you want to make a movie, or write a novel, then do it. You will quickly discover whether you really care as much about your idea as you think you do.

Some people work so hard to please everyone that they sacrifice their best ideas to draw a wider audience. This is what author David Foster Wallace called "low art," art that tries too hard to please.[28] We all know how bland bestselling books and blockbuster films can sometimes be. It's not always true, but the wider the audience you chase, the less creative your work may become. You will play to the broadest and most generic notions of what is good. How creative can something be if it appeals to everyone and disappoints no one?

---

[28] "A Conversation with David Foster Wallace by Larry McCaffery," *The Review of Contemporary Fiction*, 13.2 (Summer 1993), https://www.dalkeyarchive.com/a-conversation-with-david-foster-wallace-by-larry-mccaffery/.

It's yet another tension you will need to manage: how do you find a balance between being popular and creating something of quality (as you define it)? The best answer I've heard is from film director Steven Soderbergh, who suggested: do one project for commerce and one for art.[29] It's an interesting approach: maybe the best work can only be made if it serves only one master at a time. It's a healthy exercise to both make something entirely for yourself and entirely for other people. In each case you will stretch your boundaries for what you are capable of, as so often those conflicting desires of satisfying ourselves and satisfying other people bind us to conservative choices.

If you want to be famous for your ideas, that is a marketing problem more

---

[29] Steven Soderbergh, Keynote at the 56th San Francisco International Film Festival, http://deadline.com/2013/04/steven-soderbergh-state-of-cinema-address-486368/.

than a strictly creative one. The skill of selling ideas is different from finding and developing them. Often creators are terrible salespeople. When they try to pitch to someone, a customer or investor, they do it from their own perspective rather than first thinking carefully of the interests and demands of the person they are pitching to.

The way to solve a marketing problem is to study how to market things and invest time in building an audience for yourself, a subject well beyond the scope of this little book. I can share that it starts with simply finding one person who likes your work and then enlisting them to help you find another. With a small group of dedicated fans it's easier to attract more attention than working purely on your own. While it's true that each work you finish and release is an invitation to the world, someone still has to put those invitations in places where they can be discovered. At first this might sound demoralizing, as if you needed even more hard work to do. But if you think of marketing your work as simply another creative problem (and that you can use all the techniques you've learned so far in this book to help solve), you'll be on your way.

19. BURNOUT, BEFORE AND AFTER

The longer you work at creating things the greater the odds you'll eventually have a day where you don't feel like doing it anymore. It's hard at first to know if it's just a test of discipline: some days you won't feel like working at first, but once you start you'll feel excellent. But if you push yourself day after day and it doesn't feel right, there's probably something else going on.

Professional athletes train hard not just to perform at their best but also to help their bodies resist injuries and recover from them quickly. Creative people depend on their minds in the same way athletes depend on their bodies, and we must train our minds for the same reasons.

But how do you train your mind? There are two important ways. First is the power of will. The discipline required to finish a project really comes down to continuing to choose to work even when there are other things that, in the short term, you'd rather do. Willpower is best manifested in the skill of concentration, of being able to focus on one thing to the exclusion of others. Learning to meditate, avoiding addiction to technological devices, and developing good habits all contribute to increasing your willpower to work. Willpower behaves like a muscle, and the more you use it over time, the stronger it will become. But also like a muscle, it has its limits, and if you push it too far, it can get fatigued or injured and not work well anymore.

The second kind of training you need is emotional awareness. When you're having trouble finding motivation, you want to be able to sort through your feelings to both understand their causes and work toward a healthy state of mind that helps you. What am I feeling? Why do I feel this way? How can I let this feeling express itself so I can move on? Can I use this feeling as a motivator to work? Or do I need to get away from my current world and focus on what I'm feeling? These are all excellent questions you should be comfortable asking yourself or talking about with good friends.

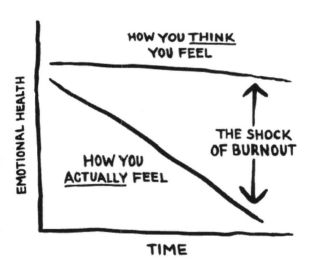

Burnout, as designer Dylan Wilbanks explains it, is a trailing indicator. This means that for weeks or months you've been taking more out of your reserves than you've put back in. Feeling burnout means there has been a problem you've ignored about how your emotions, or your mind, function, and you're finally paying the price for that oversight. Like a well of water, creative energy replenishes itself slowly over time. By the time you notice something is wrong and the well is empty, there will be no easy immediate solution.

Common signs of burnout include:

- You don't care about, or hate, the existence of the project
- Inspired, motivated, creative people annoy you
- You're drinking or eating more, or showing signs of depression
- You find it hard to relax or to concentrate

- You tore your fun socks to shreds and set them on fire

Surviving Burnout

To stay with the well example momentarily, what would you do if you literally ran out of water? Would you become one with your couch, pizza in hand, watching movies all day long, drinking massive quantities of wine, hoping for a magical creative gas to appear? I think not. You'd go out to the store, or perhaps to a neighbor's house, and ask to borrow some of theirs.

The best place to start is with friends and colleagues. Pick the one person who you relate to best and, rather than ask for feedback on your work, tell them how you feel: "Hey, can I talk to you for a minute? I'm really burned out right now." If the person you confide in cares for you, they'll listen and ask what they can do to help. They may be a good sounding board and can help you sort out what is going on. Even if the conversation is short, having your feelings validated will make you feel more normal, which in this case at least is a good thing.

If you know specifically what they can do to help, ask for it. Do you want them to try and make you laugh? Encourage you? Listen to you vent and complain? Dance outside your office door when they walk by? They can't know how to help if you don't tell them. If you work for someone, and they understand anything about creative work, it's in their interest to help you too. Even the most calculating and evil boss cares about your productivity. Let them know about your situation early, to give them more time to adjust schedules and commitments.

Survival Tactics

If creativity is personal, surviving burnout must be too. From years of collecting burnout stories and recovery methods, here are recommendations to try:

- **Plan an escape**. Take a day off and do the most dramatically easy but fun thing you can think of. Go see a matinee downtown, have a fantastic lunch, shop, browse and walk. Be as indulgent as you can stand, and if you want company, drag your friends along (and offer to return the favor when they have burnout). Use a vacation or sick day (a creative argument can be made that burnout is a form of poor mental health).
- **Scream**. Similar to my philosophy about closets, I'm a believer in primal screams. Reverting back to raw expression of a simpler state of mind helps reset my psychology. Many

people feel better after they've yelled at the top of their lungs for no particular reason, doubly so if they're upset about something. Practice different screams, such as yelling wonderful sounding words ("Papaya!") versus generic scream sounds ("Aaaaaaaagggh!"). Get friends and coworkers to participate if you can. If you're alone and have to do it into a pillow or underwater to not upset the neighbors, do it anyway. You'll feel better, I promise.

- **Fun time**. How much time per day do you make choices purely based on their quotient of fun or idle-pleasure? Why isn't this number larger? What is more important than fun and pleasure over the course of a lifetime? Whatever it is you find funny, bring more of it into your life. Choose to create more situations that are designed to bring joy.

- **Sleep and exercise**. Our minds are connected to our bodies, and if we treat our bodies poorly our minds suffer too. Start taking a walk every day. Go swimming. Have more/better sex. Free up your body, and your mind will follow.

- **Travel**. Get in the car, pick a direction and drive. Grab friends, or not. Bring food, or not. Play music really loud, or just roll down the windows and stick your head out (this is also an excellent time to practice your screams). Use vacation days if you have any, or ask for time without pay—your time away is likely more valuable than the money.

Beginning Again

After you've escaped, and let the well fill, it's time to return to work. Sometimes there's fear in approaching work again, as you worry the dread will return. Here's some advice for how to safely start again:

- **Divide projects into smaller parts**. Help yourself by focusing only on what you can do today, or in this hour. What is the smallest meaningful piece to work with? Try working on a single page. Can't do a page? Work on a paragraph. Get down to the smallest unit you can manage, but do it. After you do one piece, you might be surprised to find the next one is slightly less intimidating. If you're lucky, once a few pieces are finished, you'll discover motivation that wasn't there before. If not, just slug it out. At least you'll be able to say tomorrow you did something today.

- **Look for the worst work you can find**. Find the worst writing, the worst painting, the worst music. Force yourself to consume it. Do you feel anything? Does its existence annoy you? Make you angry? Reveal some energy in the deepest parts of your soul that you forgot was there?

Can you redirect that energy toward what you need to do today?

- **Look for the best work you can find.** Go to a museum or your favorite building. Watch your favorite film, read your favorite book. Do you get any energy from what someone you admire made? Can you bring it with you back into your own project?

20. HOW DO YOU KNOW WHEN YOU'RE DONE?

The more creative the project, the more subjective the answer is for when it's finished. In many ways, to say a project is done answers the question of "What is good?" You are saying to the world you think the work is good enough for them to experience. Accepting a project as finished means, in part, seeing its flaws (at least from the perspective of people with a different sense of goodness than yours) but accepting them as necessary to achieve its graces. A perfect work of art, if there were such a thing, would likely be perfectly boring.

Many people complained, and still complain, about the long, silent sequences in Stanley Kubrik's 2001: A Space Odyssey. Yet it's one of the most influential science fiction films of all time. Gauguin, and most of the art world, thought van Gogh's paintings were underworked and unrefined. And Gauguin was right, in a way. But given what van Gogh wanted to do, they were fantastic.

Who is right? No one is, really. The value of art is decided by two people: the artist and the viewer. Critics and experts have their say, but if you look at something and appreciate it, no one can get in your way. And if you hate it, the fact that it's famous or won awards might just make you hate it more. If you're not making art but instead building a product, you have an easier measurement of goodness: the opinions and performance of your clients and customers.

We've all read books or seen movies we didn't think were finished, or good, or worth our time. Some are simply overdone (*What Dreams May Come* isn't so much a bad film as it is a saccharine one). We forget that even the films and products we hate took years of effort by people who probably *thought* they were done. One of my favorite books is *The Old Man and the Sea*, a novel I think is one of the best ever written, yet many find it childish and overly simple. There is no one singular answer. And much of the criticism and feedback artists hear is really about the wish of the critic to describe a *different* work, not necessarily a *better* one.

Questions to ask if you're not sure if it's done:

- What were you trying to do when you started?
- Is that still what you're trying to do now?
- Is it finished, but you just don't like it anymore?

- Can you get feedback from a trusted source who matches the audience you are working for?
- Is it an effort gap: do you simply not want to do the grunt work required to finish on your good ideas?
- Do you see ways to simplify? You may have 300 pages of a great 200-page book.
- Put it away for a week or more. Then look at it with fresh eyes. How do you feel about it now?

The more works you release into the world and say "It's done!" the better your judgment will become about when something feels finished to you, the maker. And the less afraid you'll feel about handling the feedback from the world. Charles Dickens released most of his books a chapter at a time: maybe you need to work in smaller chunks of doneness (although this is easier for books and films than for paintings and sculpture). Walt Whitman simply dealt with the "is it done?" dilemma by publishing nine different versions of *Leaves of Grass* over his lifetime, each one a revision of the previous. Much like how software is often built today, he saw no reason why he couldn't keep updating it to make it better.

21. HOW TO STAY MOTIVATED

Recently I finished the sixth draft of a novel I started working on in 1994. I'm amazed myself that I've stuck with it for so long. Why do I do it? I'm not entirely sure myself! But then again, I'm often not sure why anyone does anything. Beyond the basic things we do to survive, our reasons for how we spend our time and who to spend it with are more complex than we can possibly understand. I'm motivated to work on this novel for the same reason I'm motivated to do many things: I find it interesting enough to be worthy of my time. Some people collect vinyl records, others run marathons, two things I know I'd never be motivated to do. Who is to say what is a good use of time and what is not? The only answer is you.

More practically speaking, there are certain emotional forces that you should learn to understand about yourself. If intellectually you want to spend your time finishing a project, but emotionally you're not as motivated as you need to be, there are things you can do, and that is what this last chapter is about. In the end there are seven sources of fuel for why people create the things they do.

Anger

What enrages you? What is wrong in the world, in politics, in the arts, in your workplace, in your family, and what are you going to do about it? Or will you just sit there and pretend, for another week, another year, like those others do, that it's okay? When are you going to use your feelings of frustration as fuel for doing something, anything, that brings the world a little closer to right? And don't just vent: convert rage into wonder. Use exhaust from one system to drive another. Recycle negative energy, even if it comes from your heart, and shape it into something of unmistakable goodness.

Crazy Necessity

Deliberately put yourself in situations where you have no way out but through. Sign a book deal, quit your job to make that film, buy a one-way ticket to somewhere no one you know has ever gone. While it's not advisable to gamble your life if you have dependents (families, children or your smelly dog Rupert), you'd be surprised how much support you can get for crazy necessity if you enlist support from loved ones, especially if you've been willing to do it for them. If you don't ask, or never get crazy in any way, at any time, you're the only one to blame: how can you know potential if you never test it?

Pride

Prove people wrong. They say it can't be done? Do it. They tell you it's a waste of time? Waste away. Never let anyone define for you how to be, how to use your time or what you are capable of. Turn that naysayer into a competitive guidepost, recasting every doubting Thomas into a secret twisted cheerleader. However, be careful not to decline into spite: don't center on them; they're just ammunition. Take their judgment, harness it next to your pride and ride them past the fools, over the hills and toward a dream. Have no critics? Set a goal for yourself you're not sure you can meet. Write it down, sign it, post it on your bedroom wall (with a daily discipline calendar next to it), showing it to friends and family so there's no way to sneak out the back door.

Death

If you want the most mileage out of this lifetime, then behave as if one is all you get. Spoken word artist Henry Rollins said we have infinite potential but finite time: you can't do everything, but if you choose wisely, you can do any one thing you want. Perhaps that thing won't be done as well as you'd like or earn you a living, but it can be yours in some form if you're motivated to have it before you die. Imagine yourself on your deathbed: what do you want to be able to remember? Yes, it's a cliché, but some clichés are clichés because they work. Make a list and get started. Otherwise, you deserve all your dying regrets, as you knew death was coming all along.

Fun

Know what you like. Follow what makes you laugh so hard you have to hold your ribs to breathe. It can take a lifetime to sort this out because:

- It changes as we age.
- It's hard to separate what we think we're supposed to like from what we actually enjoy.
- Many of the most fun things are cultural taboos we are afraid to break (I've shared that I like to scream the word *papaya* from car windows, and I'm sure some of my family will look at me strangely from now on).

Take time to listen to the little voice, the voice of your eight-year-old self, the voice adults, including yourself, often interrupt and speak over, and you'll rediscover what thrills you.

The Crazy Friend

Cultivate friends that say yes. Yes to midnight road trips. Yes to making silly YouTube videos. Yes to brainstorming world domination strategies over lunch. We've all known crazy friends, but after college they fade when careers, families and other mature pursuits take center stage. Yet when motivation wanes, seek out your crazy friends. They're the ones best likely to get what you're talking about, why you care so much about something few others do, and will rally behind you, increasing the odds you'll get it done. Use the buddy system: you are their crazy friend if they'll be yours.

Courage

Paul Simon said we always have something to say if we're willing to work to find it. There is a kind of courage in just showing up every day and putting in the effort.

Motivation can arise after, not before, we get started. We must expect to work and search for it. Push through fear, dig through sadness, fight through boredom and ambivalence.

It takes effort to keep going when feeling unmotivated, but that's the difference between commitment to a craft and a fantasy. And for that purpose I hope this book leads you on your way to the great things you wish to do.

-FIN-

THE

END

IT'S
REALLY
OVER

GO
AWAY
AND
CREATE
SOME
THING

HELP THE AUTHOR

Did you enjoy this book? I hope so. It took decades to write (my entire life!). Authors like me, as successful as we seem, depend on satisfied readers recommending our work to others. Can you help? It won't take more than a minute.

Please do three things right now:

1. **Write a brief review on Amazon.com**. Then share it with people you know. It's the simplest way to help attract more readers to this little book. This link will take you right there:

http://bit.ly/dance-kk

2. **Join my mailing list**. It's the best way to get news about related projects, announcements of new

works and early notice of when I'll be speaking near you. You'll get a free sampler pack with chapters from all my books just for signing up:

http://scottberkun.com/follow

3. **Recommend me for events**. I make much of my living as a keynote speaker for events and organizations. Do you know of an upcoming event and can recommend me (sample videos at the link below)? Are you organizing one? Get in touch. All of the details can be found here:

http://scottberkun.com/speaking

Thank you.

NOTES

The ambition of this book is to get you out of my thoughts and into your own as quickly as possible, so these notes are brief.

In reference to the subtitle (which claims the book is mostly honest), the only true lie is in the opening paragraph. None of the options I offered about creativity's source were real. I also offered a prize if you had the correct answer, which given that this is a book and I'm not omnipotent, it would have been impossible to provide to you even if your choice was in fact correct (a situation that was rendered impossible by the previously explained lie). Any other dishonesties found in this book are unintentional.

This book began as a talk I gave at the wonderful, but terrifyingly named, World Domination Summit in Portland, Oregon, in 2014. That talk was titled "Saving Your Creative Soul," and it was the original title for this project. My plan was to transcribe my lecture, blend in some essays on creativity I'd written before, and revise it into a short little book. This was the beginning of a very long and surprising dance of possibilities.

After various drafts, and feedback from early readers, I decided to throw out the central essay based on the talk and develop mostly new material. What had been the spine of the project was no more! Perhaps someday I'll share that abandoned 6,000 word essay as fodder for readers to examine. (Was it good? Or was I right to abandon it?) I share this anecdote with you as a testament to the preceding chapters. This is my seventh book, and every one is an adventure in a different way. No matter how many things you make, the challenge of the dance remains.

Unlike many books on creativity, I chose in this one to address the psychological challenges of starting and trying to finish projects. I was inspired by *Art & Fear: Observations on the Perils (and Rewards) of Artmaking* by David Bayles and Ted Orland, a book that has been of tremendous value in my career. I strongly recommend it over the more popular *The War of Art: Break Through the Blocks and Win Your Inner Creative Battles* by Steven Pressfield, as the latter uses metaphors (e.g. wars and battles) that aren't the most productive in my experience. However, both explore our deepest fears and attitudes about creation, and depending on your preferences, one or both will serve you well.

If you're still here reading this because you are intimidated by the blank pages of your journal and want more structure to work from, I can recommend three books. *The Doodle Revolution* by Sunni Brown, and *Draw To Win* by Dan Roam are both oriented toward business creativity, but they provide clear examples, patterns and structures you can use in many ways, including enhancing the bits of thought you put into your journal.

Auston Kleon's *The Steal Like An Artist Journal* is a solid gateway step towards having a journal of your own blank pages, with prompts, invitations and provocations to fill in with your own ideas.

The following chapters were originally published online and were heavily rewritten, many beyond recognition, for inclusion here:

- Eight (or More) Methods for Finding Ideas (based on "Creative Thinking Hacks")

- Why You Should (Learn To) Improvise (originally published as "What I Learned from Improv Class")
- The Three Gaps: Effort, Skill and Quality (based on "How To Find Your Voice")
- Why You Get Ideas (in the Shower)
- How To Be a Genius
- Don't Be Precious (with Your Ideas)
- Creativity Is Not an Accident
- What if the World Hates Your Ideas?
- What if the World Ignores Your Work?
- Burnout, Before and After (originally published as "Surviving Creative Burnout")
- How Do You Know When You're Done?
- How To Stay Motivated

ACKNOWLEDGEMENTS

Zach Gajewski and Makenzi Crouch helped with early developmental editing and thoughtful feedback. Emma Simmons led the way, as she did on *The Ghost of My Father*, with first rate copyediting of my prose.

The book cover and all drawings were done by the ever talented Tim Kordik (who also did the cover designs for two of my previous books, *Mindfire* and *The Ghost of My Father*). Thanks to Frank Chimero for permission to use his mindmap as the basis for the one used here, it's from his excellent essay "How To Have An Idea."

Thanks to my beta reader squad who read early drafts: Heather Bussing, Aimee Whitcroft, Lauren Hall-Stigerts, Rui Soares, Vanessa Longacre, Will Schroeder, Gerry Ibay, Stefan Loble, Smaranda Calin, Michael Pick, Noël Jackson, Victor Marques, Stephen

Nelson, Lizelle Herman, Ben Woelk, Radosław "Dexter" Orszewski, Neil Enns and CA Hurst.

Cheers to Clarrisa Peterson, Alyssa Fox, Anne McCarthy and Karen Davis for their laser sharp proofreading talents and generosity of time.

Special note of resplendently glorious literary recognition to my favorite escalope: Marlowe Shaeffer.

Griz, my companion for daily writing, and nighttime walking / universe pondering, a wonderfully sweet rescued Rottweiler-Labrador, passed away before this book was published. He was just a few feet away as all these words were written. Good boy, Griz. You are missed.

ABOUT THE AUTHOR

Scott Berkun is the best-selling author of books on many subjects including *The Myths of Innovation, Confessions of a Public Speaker* and *The Year Without Pants*. His work as a writer and public speaker has appeared in *The Washington Post, The New York Times, Wired Magazine, Fast Company, Forbes Magazine*, and other media. He has taught creative thinking at the University of Washington and has been a frequent commentator on CNBC, MSNBC, and National Public Radio. His popular essays and entertaining lectures are free at scottberkun.com, where you can sign up for a monthly email of all his recent and best work. He tweets at @berkun.

COLOPHON

(THE PAGE AFTER THE OTHER PAGES)

Book cover and all illustrations by
Tim Kordik

Interior book design based on the
Balance template from
BookDesignTemplates.com

Heading font: Candal
Body text font: Rosarivo
Invisible messages font:
Paradox: paradox